P9-DGH-581

The
Home Lighting
Effects Bible

YEADON PUBLIC LIBRARY
809 LONGACRE BLVD.
YEADON, PA 19050

The
Home Lighting Effects Bible

Lucy Martin

FIREFLY BOOKS

747.92
MAR

A FIREFLY BOOK

Published by Firefly Books Ltd. 2010

Copyright © 2010 Quarto Inc.

All rights reserved. No part of this publication may be reproduced, stored in a retrieval system, or transmitted in any form or by any means, electronic, mechanical, photocopying, recording or otherwise, without the prior written permission of the Publisher.

First printing

Publisher Cataloging-in-Publication Data (U.S.)
Martin, Lucy, 1968-
The home lighting effects bible / Lucy Martin.
[256] p. : ill., photos. (chiefly col.) ; cm.
Includes index.
Summary: A practical guide on how lighting can transform the home, increase the sense of space, provide practical lighting for working areas, and bring warmth, ambience, highlights, and drama.
ISBN-13: 978-1-55407-710-6
ISBN-10: 1-55407-710-9
1. Lighting, Architectural and decorative.   I. Title.
747.92 dc22   NK2115.5.L5M3785 2010

Library and Archives Canada Cataloguing in Publication
Martin, Lucy, 1968-
The home lighting effects bible / Lucy Martin.
Includes index.
ISBN-13: 978-1-55407-710-6
ISBN-10: 1-55407-710-9
      1. Lighting, Architectural and decorative. I. Title.
NK2115.5.L5M37 2010   747'.92   C2010-901406-5

Published in the United States
by Firefly Books (U.S.) Inc.
P.O. Box 1338, Ellicott Station
Buffalo, New York 14205

Published in Canada
by Firefly Books Ltd.
66 Leek Crescent
Richmond Hill, Ontario L4B 1H1

Conceived, designed and produced by

Quarto Publishing plc
The Old Brewery
6 Blundell Street
London N7 9BH
QUAR: LIB

Printed in China

10 9 8 7 6 5 4 3 2 1

Contents

PART 1

PART 2

PART 3

PART 4

PART 5

About this book 6   Introduction 8

Core knowledge 12

■ Understanding light **14**   ■ Different rooms, different requirements **16**   ■ Choosing a light source **22**
■ Energy-efficient lighting **26**   ■ Positioning light sources **28**   ■ Layering light sources **30**
■ Layering an existing lighting scheme **38**   ■ Separating the layers **40**   ■ Controlling light sources **42**

Making the most of what you've got 46

■ Harvest natural light **48**   ■ Change your bulbs **52**   ■ Change your shades **54**
■ Use plug-in solutions **58**   ■ Introduce color **60**

Principles of good lighting 62

■ Fixed recessed downlights **64**   ■ Recessed directional spotlights **70**   ■ Surface-mounted lighting **76**
■ Track lighting **82**   ■ Cable systems **86**   ■ Wall-mounted uplighting and downlighting **90**   ■ Floor-recessed uplights
and wall-recessed floor washers **96**   ■ Concealed lighting **102**   ■ Cove and coffer lighting **108**
■ Slot and niche lighting **114**   ■ Mirror lighting **118**   ■ Task lighting **124**   ■ Special effects lighting **128**

Decorative lights 134

■ Pendants **138**   ■ Ceiling-mounted fixtures **144**   ■ Wall lights **146**   ■ Floor-standing lamps **150**
■ Table lamps **154**   ■ Desk lamps **162**   ■ Kids' and fun lighting **164**   ■ Picture lights **166**   ■ Outdoor lights **168**

In the home 170

■ Front doors and porches **172**   ■ Entrances and hallways **174**   ■ Stairs and landings **178**   ■ Living rooms **184**
■ Kitchens **188**   ■ Dining rooms **192**   ■ Open-plan living **196**   ■ Children's rooms **200**   ■ Home offices **202**
■ Wine cellars **206**   ■ Media rooms **208**   ■ Half baths **212**   ■ Bedrooms **214**   ■ Bathrooms **218**
■ Home gyms **224**   ■ Swimming pools **226**   ■ Sunrooms **230**   ■ Outdoor spaces **234**   ■ Details **240**

■ Glossary **246**   ■ Resources **248**   ■ Index **252**   ■ Credits **256**

About this book

It has never been more important to choose your light sources with care. Good lighting will pull a home decor scheme together, but where should you begin? This book explains the technical know-how you need and the aesthetic judgments you have to make to ensure your lighting schemes work in the different rooms in your home. Throughout each of the five parts of the book you will find information that helps guide your choices, backed up by photographs of inspirational examples of a wide variety of lighting fixtures and schemes.

PART 1: CORE KNOWLEDGE

In part 1 of this book you will learn the basic differences between the most common types of light sources: standard domestic-voltage lightbulbs, low-voltage lightbulbs, LEDs and fluorescent lights. Once you have a better understanding of the effects of different types of light sources, you can use your knowledge to plan different types of lighting to suit different rooms, and you will begin to understand how to layer and control lighting to create depth, texture and atmosphere.

PART 2: MAKING THE MOST OF WHAT YOU'VE GOT

You can begin to improve the lighting in your home with even the smallest of budgets. Part 2 is packed with a wealth of ideas to help you maximize what you already have, without the help of an electrician. You can change the bulbs you use, exploit daylight, use plug-in solutions, change the shape, color and texture of your lamp shades, introduce color or dim your light sources.

PART 3: PRINCIPLES OF GOOD LIGHTING

If you have the luxury of starting from scratch, part 3 will help you design superb lighting schemes, starting with the basics. The main types of lighting and the fixtures employed for that purpose are described, and the author provides advice on the situations in which each can be used most effectively.

PART 4: DECORATIVE LIGHTS

Lighting fixtures often serve a far broader function than simply providing illumination to a space; they are a key decorative element. Lighting fixtures have a major impact on a space and are inextricably linked with the style of a room. They are also an ideal way to put a personal stamp on a scheme. In part 4 you will find a gallery of light fixtures — categorized by application and broad style grouping — to suit a wide range of tastes and requirements, which will help inspire your choices.

PART 5: IN THE HOME

Finally, part 5 shows you how all of these elements can be knitted together in the different living spaces of a home. These examples illustrate how combined architectural and decorative lighting solutions create discreet or eye-catching schemes that complement and enhance any interior and help you create the home of your dreams.

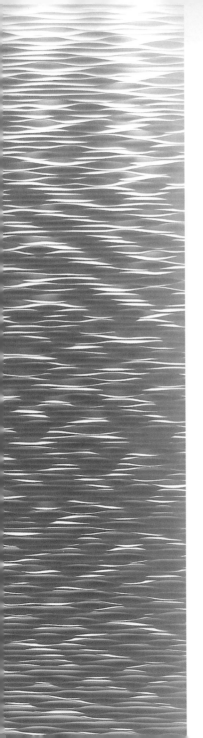

Introduction

Light plays a pivotal role in our lives, often without our being aware of it. Altering lighting will transform a space, and even the simplest scheme will have a surprisingly dramatic impact. How you light your home is as important as how you choose to decorate it. Many of us spend a lot of time and effort on the decorative scheme, but fewer spend much time considering lighting.

The magic of light
Lighting can be confusing because it is not something you can physically get hold of. Its effect is hard to judge as it changes depending on where you put it and what surrounds it. But looked at from another point of view, that is also the magic of light. The same fixture and bulb can have either little impact (a single downlight in the middle of a room) or make a strong impression (a single downlight in a niche) depending on how and where you use it.

Lighting for the future
New types of light sources are constantly being developed. The need for energy efficiency was the major catalyst in the

evolution of available light sources and the design of light fixtures. In the not-so-distant past, the low-voltage bulb was revolutionary because it offered a physically smaller but nonetheless powerful light source, but nowadays new energy-saving forms of light such as light emitting diodes (LEDs) and organic LEDs (OLEDs) are propelling lighting technology into a new era. The development of such light sources is moving quickly, and it is important for anyone working with light to keep up to date with the best products available. Clever combinations of "old" and "new" light sources will give you desirable lighting and atmosphere and provide you with improved energy efficiency and ease of maintenance.

The fundamentals of good lighting

The best lighting schemes look effortless. If a space is lit well, it will be attractive and inviting. Rooms that are well lit get used, but poorly lit rooms are often abandoned. If you understand the different light sources available and the different

requirements for different rooms, you can begin to wield your "lighting toolbox" with confidence. You will then be able to select, position and layer your lighting wisely. It is worth remembering that the best schemes usually employ less rather than more light.

Once you have the key lights in place, the next step is to control the lighting levels, either to create practical amounts of light for work or to provide low levels of light for mood. Simple manipulation of the fixed light sources is the key to successful multifunctional spaces. The underlying aim is to provide the appropriate levels of light for a variety of different purposes and at different times of day.

Using reflection

When deciding what type of lighting to use and where to put it, remember that light travels in a straight line. If you want an even, shadow-free light — for example, in a playroom or home office — use a wall-mounted uplight or a concealed light on top of a high-level unit. Light from such fixtures will rise and reflect off the ceiling.

Dramatic lighting
Good lighting and dramatic effects do not have to be complicated. A simple downlight creates depth and texture in this niche, turning a single bloom into a work of art.

The importance of shadow

Shadow and shade are just as important as light in a successfully lit interior. A room with no shadow can look "bleached out" and lacking in texture. Sometimes it is important to have an even illumination, such as in an office. However, atmosphere and mood are built by pacing light throughout a space; positioning it where it is needed to draw the eye around the room.

Light and mood

Remember that we respond to light in an emotional way. For example, some forms of light can make you feel comfortable and cozy—for instance, lamp light in a living room—or active and vibrant, as in a brightly lit kitchen. Thus, light has the power to alter your mood. If in doubt about how to tackle the lighting in a particular space, ask yourself how you want people to feel when spending time in that room.

Lighting for all requirements
Every room responds differently to the lights placed within it depending on its shape, size and function. Apply the fundamentals of good lighting to provide a template for building a lighting scheme for airy, open-plan spaces or cozy, texture-filled rooms. Employ classic designs, such as the Atollo lamp by Vico Magistretti (left), or embrace future-proofed LED solutions, such as the LED Mathmos Aduki beans (below), to bring your home to life.

Core
knowledge

PART **1**

- Understanding light
- Different rooms, different requirements
- Choosing a light source
- Energy-efficient lighting
- Positioning light sources
- Layering light sources
- Layering an existing lighting scheme
- Separating the layers
- Controlling light sources

Core knowledge about lighting in your home includes the principles of good lighting and the variety of light sources available. Once you understand the effects of different types of lightbulbs and how each affects different textures—for example, of walls and floors—you can begin to build a lighting scheme that works well. A good lighting scheme involves the correct choice of light source, positioning it to best effect, combining it cleverly with other types of light, layering it to provide you with flexibility and, finally, controlling it to maximize its usefulness and impact.

Understanding light

How do you understand something if you can only see the effect and can't touch or hold it? Light comes from either a primary light source or as reflected light from an illuminated object or surface.

As our eyes are always drawn to the brightest point, we can use light to make a small space appear larger. This also means that a well-positioned light — for example, to light a picture over a mantelpiece — will have a dramatic impact. We will see this image more strongly than the less well-lit areas around it.

Using reflection
When deciding what kind of light to use and where to put it, remember that light travels in a straight line. If you want even, shadow-free light—for example, in a playroom or home office — use a wall-mounted uplight or a concealed light on top of a high unit. This light will rise upward and reflect off the ceiling, creating diffused light.

Light will bounce off mirrors at the same angle at which it hits them. This is critical to ensure an even light to a face in a bathroom mirror, for example. Using a directional spotlight as opposed to a straight downlight to light a mirror always provides a better light to a face.

The importance of shadow
Shadow and shade are just as important as the light in a successfully lit interior. A room with no shadow can look "bleached out" and lacking in texture. Sometimes it is important to have an even illumination, such as in an office space. However, atmosphere and mood are built by placing light sources throughout

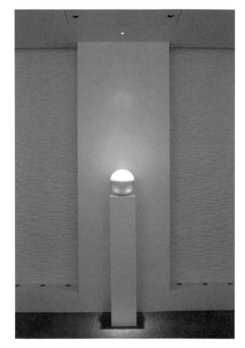

Direct approach
The ceiling-recessed downlight is positioned directly over the object to be lit. It creates a strong light on top of the sphere and produces a corresponding shadow.

Ceiling-recessed downlight

a space—in other words, positioning them where they are needed to draw the eye around the room.

◀ Enhanced depth
A miniature downlight creates crisp highlights over both the artwork and the orchid beneath. Placing the light in the niche helps to create a greater sense of space in the small bathroom by drawing the eye to the object on display.

Light and mood
Remember that we respond to light in an emotional way. For example, some forms of light can make you feel comfortable and cozy—for instance, lamp light in a living room — or active and vibrant, as in a brightly lit kitchen. If in doubt about how to tackle lighting in a particular space, ask yourself how you want people to feel when they are in that room.

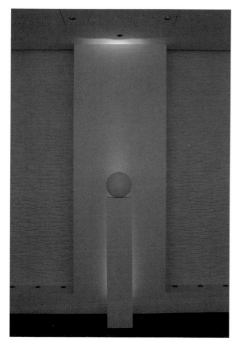

Hidden drama
A surface-mounted uplight positioned at floor level behind the object throws it into silhouette. This creates a restful focal point and provides depth to the space.

Hidden uplight

Maximum impact
A pair of directional spotlights positioned in front of the object at the correct distance from the wall cast a wide wash of light, flattening the object.

Directional-recessed spotlights

Different rooms, different requirements

Practical light is needed in nearly every room in a house, to enable you to see what you are doing. But the function of a room dictates what type of lighting will be most suitable. Part 5 details how to make the most of different rooms, and this section introduces the principles of lighting the primary spaces in a home.

Think carefully about the use for which the room is intended; is it primarily a practical space in which you need a good level of working light, or is the room principally a space for relaxation and social interaction? Your scheme will need to provide the best lighting for the intended use.

■ A hallway should feel welcoming. Pendant lights and table lamps or wall lights provide that ambience.

■ A living room works best with layered lighting that caters to different uses at different times of day. Ceiling-recessed lights to illuminate focal points and draw the eye around the space will enhance the sense of room and light mirrors and artwork. Lighting blinds, shutters or curtain areas prevents large blank spots at night, when these are closed. Table or standard lamps are essential for a cozy atmosphere. A small number of large lamps works best.

■ In a kitchen, lamp light, wall lights and focal-point lighting, such as a dramatic or pretty pendant, will all enhance a room in which you spend a great deal of time, but

Welcome pairing

A pair of tall table lamps provide a welcoming light in the hallway and also serve to frame the mirror. The eye is drawn to the first landing, where recessed downlights wash the walls, and to the rear of the hallway, where they are used to light flowers on a table.

Ceiling-recessed downlight

Table lamps

Large lamps
frame the
elevation

Low-voltage
spotlights on
beams wash light
over wall

Table lamp by
seating for cozy
light

Ideal lights for
intermediate light

Layered light

The layers of light used in this living room help to create a
cozy atmosphere while still highlighting the textured stone
wall. Surface-mounted spotlights sit on beams (unseen) to
wash light down the natural stone and enhance the color
and texture of the wall. Wall lights provide an intermediate
light, and lamps frame the dominant elevation and provide
a warm light by the seating.

that also needs to be highly practical. It is easy to avoid working in your own shadow by the use of well-positioned ceiling-recessed lights that give you shadow-free light.

■ A dining room needs to be lit at an intermediate height. Wall lights and picture lights as well as table lamps are obvious choices. You can achieve sufficient lighting around the table with directional spotlights or hanging pendants, or a combination of the two. Cross-lighting a glass chandelier with a low-voltage spotlight will increase the reflections and enhance its sparkle.

■ Bedrooms actually need very little light most of the time. However, practical light levels are needed for cleaning and tasks such as packing. This can be provided by a combination of wall lights and discreet overhead lighting that can be dimmed for ambience. Good bedside reading lights are key. This may mean installing a specific

Ceiling-recessed downlight

Wall-mounted light

Mini spotlight

Wall light

▲ Elegant practicality
A good spread of even light is achieved over the island unit in this kitchen by the use of ceiling-recessed directional spotlights, providing an easy, practical light for food preparation.

▶ Relaxed dining
The stylish wall lights serve to create a relaxed atmosphere in this dining room and frame the far elevation, pulling an otherwise blank wall together. The mini spotlights, semi-recessed in the skylight, throw a sparkle up into the glass and prevent the glass panes from appearing black and gloomy at night.

reading light such as a wall-mounted flexible LED as well as a substantial lamp on a bedside table.

■ The bathroom needs a practical, shadow-free light that enables you to see clearly. But mood lighting is equally important, now that bathrooms are becoming more of a place for relaxation. This is often achieved by introducing lights in niches or with the use of low-level floor fixtures.

■ In a playroom, wall-mounted incandescent uplights or up/down lights give a bright, even light. It is a good idea to install dimmers for the times when you need less light. This does away with the clutter—and perhaps danger for small children—of floor or table lamps.

■ The utility room is a great place to use energy-efficient lighting. Bright, clean, compact fluorescent lighting in wall-mounted units or daylight-white fluorescent bulbs positioned on top of wall-mounted or full-height units is usually all that you need.

Directional spotlights

Laid-back luxury
In this restful bedroom, dimmed ceiling-recessed directional spotlights highlight the silk headboard, but when used at full strength they provide practical lighting in the wardrobe.

■ In a study or home office, effective task lighting is vital. In a large study, where a desk is placed in the center of the room, a well-placed floor socket for a desk light is essential to avoid trailing wires. Lighting within shelving adds to overall light levels and makes a space feel larger. In a compact desk area, task lighting can be wall mounted or positioned under cabinets or shelves above the desk.

Jeweled delight

Lighting within the niches gives a soft sidelight and adds a moody evening ambience to this bathroom. The mirror is backlit with an LED strip, providing a contemporary feel — an ideal way to light a mirror when space is tight.

Visual feast

Transform your bathroom into a relaxing haven by using hidden light sources. Floor-recessed uplights define architectural details. Top lighting in the niches displays the objects placed within them.

Choosing a light source

There is a huge variety of lightbulbs and other light sources available. However, knowing what to expect from a particular light source in terms of output (often measured in lumens), color characteristics, lifespan and energy efficiency is not always easy and demands a certain amount of technical knowledge.

▶ **Understanding color temperature**
Color temperature, measured in kelvins (K), is a characteristic of visible light. Temperatures of 5,000K or more are called cool colors, while temperatures of less than 3,000K are described as warm.

Types of light sources

The main types of light sources—one of the key areas of knowledge for any newcomer to lighting design—are described in this section. Energy-efficient lighting is discussed in detail on pages 26–27.

Banned bulbs

In the U.S. a law has been enacted that requires that general-purpose incandescent bulbs between 40 and 100 watts become 30 percent more efficient. By 2012, 100-watt bulbs must meet this standard, while 40-watt bulbs have until 2014. In Canada there are plans to ban inefficient bulbs by 2012.

Incandescent

This was, until recently, the most common type of incandescent mains electricity bulb worldwide and produces a wonderfully soft, warm and atmospheric light when dimmed. Available in many wattages and cap styles and sizes, they are cheap to make, inexpensive to buy and commonly used in table lamps, floor lamps and pendants. However, approximately 90 percent of the power consumed by an incandescent lightbulb is emitted as heat rather than visible light, and they typically need replacing after approximately 2,000 hours of use.

Comparison of output for incandescent and fluorescent light sources

Incandescent	Fluorescent	Minimum light
40 watts	9 to 13 watts	415 lumens
60 watts	13 to 15 watts	800 lumens
75 watts	18 to 25 watts	900–950 lumens
100 watts	26 to 30 watts	1,340 lumens

Incandescent bulbs

Most incandescent bulbs are available with screw caps.

Standard   Halogen energy-saving bulb   Spotlight   Standard candle bulb   Flicker candle bulb   Squirrel-cage bulb

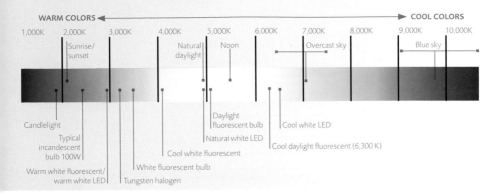

WARM COLORS ◄ ─────────────────────────────────► COOL COLORS

| 1,000K | 2,000K | 3,000K | 4,000K | 5,000K | 6,000K | 7,000K | 8,000K | 9,000K | 10,000K |

Sunrise/sunset — Natural daylight — Noon — Overcast sky — Blue sky

Candlelight
Typical incandescent bulb 100W
Warm white fluorescent/warm white LED
White fluorescent bulb
Tungsten halogen
Cool white fluorescent
Daylight fluorescent bulb
Natural white LED
Cool white LED
Cool daylight fluorescent (6,300 K)

Fluorescent

Fluorescent tubes are again becoming more popular, as we seek more energy-efficient forms of lighting. Both compact fluorescents (see page 26) and fluorescent tubes are energy efficient in that they combine high light output with low power consumption. Typically, those used in the home emit only around 30 percent of their energy in heat, making them far cooler and more energy efficient than regular incandescent bulbs. Linear fluorescent bulbs can be dimmed with the right fixtures, and dimmable compact versions are now available.

From watts to lumens

Watts as the standard unit for describing the "strength" of bulbs is gradually being phased out and being replaced by lumens. The chart below provides a conversion from wattage to lumens for each of the main types of bulb.

Incandescent		Fluorescent		Compact fluorescent		Linear halogen	
watts	lumens	watts	lumens	watts	lumens	watts	lumens
40	415	14	800	11	900	100	1,600
60	710			18	1,200	150	2,500
100	1,340			26	1,800	200	3,500
				42	3,200		

Seeing color

Fluorescent strip lights are commonly available in warm white, daylight white and cool white. Daylight white is an excellent choice if you need to provide light inside a wardrobe or closet. You will be able to see a clear difference between your black, navy blue and brown clothing. Used with colored gel sleeves (see page 60), they are also an easy and cheap way to inject a dramatic and intense punch of saturated color into a lighting scheme.

Fluorescent lamps

Standard fluorescent tube

Compact fluorescent bulbs
Fluorescent bulbs are available in compact energy-saving forms that are becoming more widespread. See pages 26–27 for more information.

Single- and double-ended halogen

The single- and double-ended halogen bulb is typically found in wall-mounted uplights. The long, thin tungsten filament is surrounded by halogen gas to make the light that is emitted much whiter. This is ideal for situations where you need a wide spread of reflected light that, unlike a fluorescent strip, will provide a soft, atmospheric glow when dimmed. This is a really useful light source in playrooms, home offices and kitchens. Energy-saving versions are available.

Low-voltage halogen

Requiring a transformer, typical low-voltage halogen bulbs make colors seem fresher than incandescent bulbs do. They can provide either a diffuse, shadow-free illumination or a sharply defined, narrow beam. They are useful for both accent and general lighting applications. It is worth investing in good-quality bulbs. These will typically last longer (around 5,000 hours) and produce a truer color rendition than cheaper versions. Low-voltage halogen lamps are available in different beam widths: from 10 to 60 degrees. Used skilfully, these bulbs can fulfill a huge number of lighting tasks in your home. Softening, sandblasted and linear lenses are also available to "diffuse" and "stretch" the hard arc of light to make it appear softer (see page 67).

Standard-voltage halogen

Standard-voltage halogen bulbs produce more light than a standard incandescent bulb of the same wattage, but they are as inefficient as the standard bulb. They are comparatively expensive to run and to buy, and they generate a lot of heat. They are dimmable and available in a number of beam widths. Because of their disadvantages, standard-voltage halogen bulbs are likely to be substituted with more economic light sources.

Double-ended halogen

3 1/8 inch (76 mm) double-ended halogen

4 11/16 inch (117 mm) double-ended halogen

Low-voltage halogen

Typical MR16 dichroic bulb

Black-backed MR16 dichroic bulb

Silver-backed MR16 dichroic bulb

Aluminum reflector halogen

Open-fronted MR16 dichroic bulb

Standard-voltage halogen

Standard-voltage halogen bulb

Looking to the future

Organic light-emitting diodes (OLEDs) are solid-state devices composed of thin films of organic molecules that create light with the application of electricity. At present they are mainly used in electronic devices to provide crisp displays. They use significantly less power than conventional LEDs and have huge potential for lighting in the future.

LED

Found in all sorts of devices, the light-emitting diode (LED) is basically just a tiny chip that fits easily into an electronic circuit. LEDs don't have filaments and therefore don't get hot and won't burn out. A high percentage of the electrical power goes directly to generate the light, cutting down considerably on electricity demands. They require a driver (a power supply that provides a constant voltage appropriate to the LED) and at present may be more expensive than incandescent bulbs, but they are more efficient to run. They can appear as single light sources, as in a floor-recessed uplight, where their cool temperature is an advantage. However, in the form of a linear light source, LEDs are revolutionizing lighting in the home. Linear LED light is almost as thin as adhesive tape and this thinness combined with its coolness means it can be used in shelves and coves.

Fiber-optic system

A light box contains the bulb (usually incandescent or metal halide) and projects the light down a glass or plastic fiber until it appears at the fiber's end. The fiber end can be anywhere—for example, up in a high ceiling or cast into a concrete wall or steps. The ability to separate the light output from the location of the electrical supply has obvious safety and maintenance advantages. Fiber optics are commonly used to create starry sky effects—for example, in a roof over a swimming pool or hot tub or as a night-light over a child's bed. It is also a great way to introduce color, as color "wheels" can be inserted into the light box to create a solid color or an ever-changing array of colors. This effect can be very dramatic when used as uplights to wash a white wall with different hues. There is a distance limitation of about 20 feet (6 m) between the fiber end and the light box.

LED

LED chips fitted within a single light source

Linear LED

Fiber optic

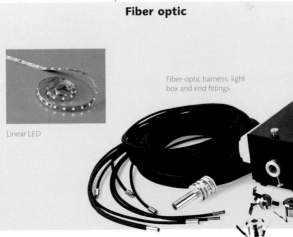

Fiber-optic harness, light box and end fittings

Energy-efficient lighting

The development of light sources is now driven by the need for energy efficiency. Most of us wish to reduce our energy consumption, but the pace of change has left many people confused about their options. The key is to try out these options and see which suits your needs the best.

There are three main options for replacing standard-voltage incandescent bulbs in the home: energy-efficient compact fluorescent (CF) bulbs; energy-saving halogen bulbs, some of which are also designed to look like conventional bulbs; and LED bulbs.

IRC bulbs

You can find many bulbs with an infrared coating (IRC) that further reduces energy consumption. An IRC equivalent of the 150-watt linear incandescent lamp typically used in uplights draws only 120 watts, and an IRC equivalent of a typical low-voltage 50-watt spotlight draws only 35 watts. These bulbs may not be fully energy-efficient, but they do provide some energy savings and provide an equivalent light output.

The color of light provided by different light sources

Not energy efficient   Energy efficient

Energy-efficient bulbs

Stick-shaped CF bulb

The light emitted by compact fluorescent energy-efficient bulbs (CF) is often grayer than that produced by traditional incandescent lamps. Although many bulbs within this category cannot be used with a dimmer, some manufacturers are now offering dimmable versions as well. When dimmed, however, the light source does not change color (for instance, becoming warmer), it just reduces the amount of light emitted. Some have enclosed the light source in frosted plastic coatings to soften the light.

Pros
■ They offer energy savings of up to 80 percent over incandescent equivalents.
■ They have a long life, lasting for 10,000 to 20,000 hours, depending on the type and manufacturer.

Cons
■ Dimming options may be limited.
■ Compact fluorescent bulbs contain small amounts of mercury and cannot be discarded in your household garbage. They must be taken to a CF bulb recycling center.

Candle CF bulb

Twist or spiral CF bulb

Classic-shaped CF bulb

▶ **Energy-efficient color**
Colorful shades are a great way of disguising compact fluorescent light sources. This solution is great for playrooms, hallways and utility rooms.

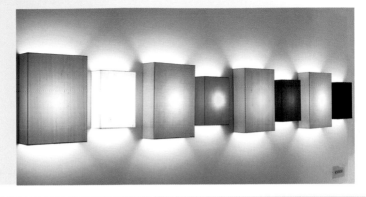

Energy-saving bulbs

These look very similar to the old incandescent bulbs, for which they are a direct replacement. Inside the bulb, there is no filament in the traditional sense. Instead, manufacturers use a combination of IRC (infrared coating) and the inert gas xenon to help retain heat. Thus, more of the available energy is used to provide light. These bulbs dim beautifully on standard dimmers, allowing you to create a warm tone.

Pros
■ They produce a light similar to traditional bulbs.
■ They have a truer color rendering than energy-efficient bulbs.
■ They are fully dimmable.
■ They contain no mercury and do not require special disposal.

Cons
■ They offer less energy savings than energy-efficient bulbs; they are only 30 percent more energy efficient than an equivalent incandescent bulb.

LEDs

A typical LED is in the form of a "chip." These are often put into a classic incandescent bulb design. This new technology gives more visible light for the same amount of electrical input and generates much less heat. LED bulbs are available in white and colored versions. A white 3-watt LED can replace a 15-watt standard incandescent bulb, and a colored 1- to 1.8-watt version can replace a standard colored 25-watt bulb. A color change version (over a 2-minute cycle) is also available. With wattage as low as 1 to 1.8, LED bulbs consume very little power, but at present they are not suitable for use with dimmers. In spite of technological advances, LEDs are still a long way from being satisfactory replacements for standard household bulbs.

Pros
■ Provide an energy saving of up to 80 percent over standard incandescent equivalents.
■ Exceptionally durable and resistant to breakage and vibrations.
■ Produce little heat.
■ A possible life of around 25 years, depending on usage.

Cons
■ Output is insufficient to be truly practical.
■ Color rendition is not true.

Positioning light sources

When deciding on where to position light sources in any scheme, you first need to consider the function of the room and then decide what type of lighting would work best. Do you need practical lighting, task lighting, highlighting or atmosphere—or a combination of all these elements?

Sometimes it is hard to decide how you want a room to work for you, particularly if the space has to combine several different functions. This is when a professional eye can be invaluable. A good lighting designer will be able to "read" the room, understand your requirements and translate your needs into practical solutions.

Light layers
This cozy living room combines dramatic hanging pendants, a cleverly uplit fireplace and warm lamp light. The paintings are beautifully highlighted with ceiling-recessed spotlights.

Wall-mounted downlights

Buried uplights

Spiked LED spotlights

▲ Reflected texture

The lighting works to highlight the multiple textures and layers of this patio garden. Uplights buried in the ground and flexible LED spotlights spiked into the flower beds display the planting, while the walls are washed with light by simple wall-mounted downlights.

Ceiling-recessed spotlights

Wall lights

Floor washers

▲ Gentle procession

Ceiling-recessed directional spotlights highlight the pictures in this hallway, creating pace as the eye moves from one focal point to the next. Wall lights and low-level floor washers complete the effect.

Layering light sources

The rooms you live in are three-dimensional, so you need to approach your lighting with this in mind. Layering your lighting will enable you to create a more visually textured space, and it will provide more depth and atmosphere than you can obtain using a single light source.

Once you have understood the effects created by different light sources, you can begin to plan different light layers. Remember that lights do not always have to be recessed within or hung from a ceiling. Think about how you might make use of the walls, the floor and even furniture as places in and on which to locate light sources. Light sources can be positioned in or on ceilings, on walls at high, mid or low level and may also be recessed into floors or walls at low level.

Light layering in action

A simple example of light layering can be seen in a child's bedroom. It can be functionally lit with a central pendant that provides a certain amount of practical light and can also be dimmed. However, the simple addition of a bedside light or freestanding floor lamp by a reading chair will open out the sense of space and will create a warmer, cozier atmosphere.

Good, basic lighting combines a single high-level light source in the ceiling for practical illumination with lighting at a lower level, provided by table or floor-standing lamps. Already this combination gives you more ways in which you can use the room. The ceiling lighting gives you practical light for the daytime, and the lamp light provides atmosphere in the evening. If you fit dimmers to both light sources, you will produce further combinations — for example, in the evening

you can choose to dim the overhead light and have the lamp light brighter for relaxed reading or watching television.

Practical and atmospheric

Dining rooms provide a good example of how the layered lighting approach can transform a space. In a dining room, people are generally seated around a table. Obviously light is required over the table, but because people are seated, lighting needs to be generated at lower levels within the room. Wall lights and picture lights are an excellent way to insert light at a lower level and create a more intimate atmosphere.

In a bathroom, layering helps to provide appropriate lighting for different tasks. It is important to achieve good lighting to the face when using the mirror, and a correctly positioned overhead light is essential. This illuminates the face as the light bounces back from the mirror, but it also creates shadows. The introduction of a mid layer of light in the form of wall lights mounted on the mirror or on either side of it provides in-fill light that evens out skin tone and eliminates shadows.

▶ **Sketch it**
Sketching out your ideas will help you to consolidate your thoughts. And, no matter how rough your drawings, they will provide a helpful starting point for your discussions with your lighting designer or electrician.

▲ Filling the void
Clever use of a linear light source under the
coffee table creates a floating effect, while
the floor-mounted uplights illuminate the
structural supports.

Wall washers

Linear light
source

Floor-based uplights

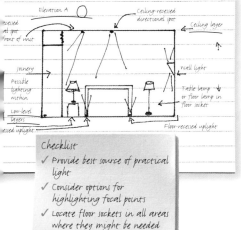

Checklist
✓ Provide best source of practical
  light
✓ Consider options for
  highlighting focal points
✓ Locate floor sockets in all areas
  where they might be needed

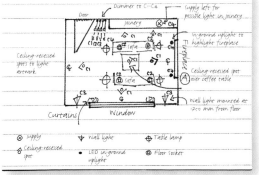

Planned approach

The following sequence of lighting diagrams shows how the lighting scheme in a kitchen (shown on pages 33–37) is laid out informally in a lighting plan. The symbols are colored to indicate how the various layers are built up to create lighting in a multipurpose kitchen, suitable for the practicalities of food preparation as well as creating the right ambience for entertaining.

First lighting layer

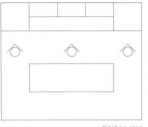

Kitchen plan

Elevation of island unit

Second lighting layer

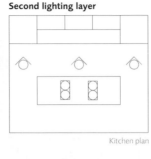

Kitchen plan

Elevation of island unit

Key

⬡	Ceiling-recessed directional spotlight
◯	Ceiling-recessed fixed spotlight
▯	Ceiling-recessed fixed spotlight
⊖	Recessed under-cabinet LED
✳	Chandelier
⊡	LED floor washer
⊠	Miniature LED floor washer
-□-□-□-	Linear LED
├───┤	Fluorescent tubes

Third/fourth lighting layer

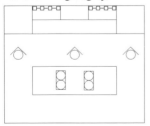

Kitchen plan

Elevation of island unit

Fifth lighting layer

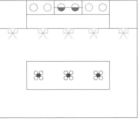

Kitchen plan

Elevation of island unit

Sixth lighting layer

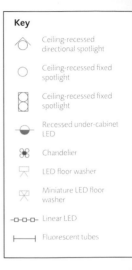

Kitchen plan

Elevation of island unit

1 Lighting the countertops

Use correctly positioned directional spotlights in the ceiling to highlight kitchen countertops. Set the fixtures in line with the edge of the counter so that you do not cast a shadow over the area where you are working. Directional light gives a you a good level of light without glare.

Directional spotlights

2 Lighting the island

Add practical light to the island work surface with ceiling-recessed or surface-mounted downlights. Use different beam widths to create different effects: a narrow beam for highlights and a medium and wide beam for in-fill or working light.

Low-glare spotlights

4 **Lighting the structure**
Consider what lighting you can put into the structure of the kitchen itself, such as backlighting glass shelves to highlight objects on display. This will soften the space and help to blur the boundary between the functionality of a kitchen and the relaxed atmosphere of a living room or dining room.

3 **Under-cabinet lighting**
Task light in the form of under-cabinet lighting introduces a layer of light at a lower level while providing a local work light when you do not want to use overhead lighting.

Shelf lighting

Under-cabinet LEDs

For extra sparkle, small glass pendants are hung from the center fixture over the counter.

5 Lighting the front of the island

Use a concealed linear light source to wash light down the front of an island. This will make the unit seem less "solid" in the space and link it with the rest of the kitchen. In a combined kitchen–dining room, it also provides a soft light to create the right ambience for dining. Low-level lights in the kick plate skim the floor, enhance color and texture and contribute to the mood lighting.

Decorative pendant

Linear LEDs

Low-level floor washers

6 High- and low-level lighting and color

Concealed linear lighting on top of wall units can be dimmed for soft light at night (as shown here) or turned up for shadow-free reflected light when working in the kitchen. Linear lighting along the kick plates on the rear wall provides more subtle light, adding depth and interest at floor level. A color-changing LED set behind the glass backsplash adds a touch of drama to suit your mood.

Concealed linear lighting

Color-changing LED

Linear light

Layering an existing lighting scheme

In many cases, you can easily adapt an existing lighting scheme to create layered lighting. Layering can be achieved by inserting light sources into or onto objects such as furniture or shelving. This approach is often useful for improving light in a room when you are not able to start from scratch.

If you have a room that is lit by only one light source, try adding a light into a piece of furniture such as a bookshelf or display unit. This option is also useful in small spaces. In a living room—where lamp light placed at a low level is really essential for atmosphere— where little floor space is available, lights under cabinets in display units can transform

Fluorescent tubes

Under-cabinet lights

◀ **Retro solutions**
This kitchen, in an historic building, offered the opportunity to build light into a space where it was not possible to use any recessed lighting in the ceiling. Linear fluorescent lights sit on top of the cabinet, and under-cabinet lighting gives good working light to the countertops.

▶ **Plug the gap**
Boost light levels and add a diffused uplight to a space with a plug-in incandescent floor-based uplight. This is a great way to lift light levels when you are not able to rewire a space.

the space. In this situation the light will function in a similar way to the table or floor lamp, but without creating clutter. In a room lit only by lamp light, adding light sources under shelves, into window ledges or on top of units to light books or objects will add to the general light level and provide you with additional flexibility and more depth.

Low-voltage uplights

Wall lights

Pendant fixture

Minimum disruption
Low-voltage uplights can be wired into the window ledge to highlight the window. The existing supplies in the ceiling and on the walls were used for a neutral pendant and wall lights in the same color as the walls.

Tips for emphasizing features

■ Layering lights also allows you to make the most of any architectural features in a room, especially in historic buildings, where you may not want to disturb the fabric of the building.
■ Use a simple floor-based plug-in uplight (left) if a fitted solution is not an option, to provide visual focus and eliminate dark corners.

■ Use recessed uplights in the floor to highlight architraves, archways and fireplaces.
■ Add lighting to niches in a bathroom or shower. This not only serves a useful purpose for display or storage, but it also provides depth and atmosphere and keeps any ceiling lighting requirements to a minimum.

■ Highlight treasured objects with the use of a plug-in tabletop spotlight. Easy to manipulate, this type of miniature fitting can be moved to suit.

Separating the layers

Be sure to give yourself maximum flexibility by keeping the different layers of lighting on separate circuits. This will allow you to choose how much or how little of each layer you want to use at any one time. Some useful examples of these principles in action are described here.

Open-plan living spaces

The practical lighting for a kitchen, to light countertops and islands, is often found in the ceiling. Low-level light can be introduced by means of floor "washers" fitted into the kick plates of the cabinets and by lights under wall units to provide local, working light to the work surfaces.

The dining area needs good light to the table and low-level lights, such as wall lights, to provide ambiance while seated. The family room will benefit from lamps for light while

seated and good illumination of focal points. If you have these light sources on separate circuits, you can choose different lighting setups, according to how the room is being used, and avoid the waste of lights being on when not needed. For example, while you are dining you can leave just a small amount of light on in the kitchen for practical reasons, and this will also ensure that the space is not "lost" when not in use.

Double-height spaces

The same approach can be used to great effect in any double-height space. The key is to enhance any special features in the upper areas but also to provide light at lower levels.

A pitched roof can be lit using uplights placed on the tops of beams or by spotlights fixed to beams. A mezzanine level should have lighting on the same circuit as the main

Low-level floor washers

Wall-mounted up/down light

Floor-recessed LED uplight

Light reunion

This hall has three visible layers of lighting: under the stairs, on the stairs and on the wall by the door. By wiring these three circuits separately, it is easy to combine separate layers or to have them at separate intensities to create different moods.

Setting the scene

Multiple layers are employed in this kitchen/living area to create the potential for four different scenes: day, afternoon, evening and late evening. Layers can be left in a "scene" or turned off to provide just the right amount of light required.

Ceiling-recessed light
Lamp light

Low-glare ceiling-recessed spotlights
Ceiling-recessed lights

room to keep the areas visually connected. In lofts, stairways and split-level apartments, if one area can be seen from another, in terms of lighting, you should treat these as one area, not as separate spaces. Use the lighting to delineate the spaces, and use thoughtful circuiting to provide flexibility.

Controlling light sources

Most light sources are simply switched on and off. However, to maximize the effects you can achieve with a fixed light source, you also need to be able to dim it, and there are a number of ways you can do this.

Manual dimming

A manual dimmer using a rotary motion allows you to adjust the light level to suit the time and day and the purpose of the room. It is the simplest way to provide flexibility in your lighting. The actual element that allows a circuit to dim is the "dimmer module," which is concealed in the back box behind the face plate. A standard dimmer allows you to dim from one point only on a circuit. Therefore, if you have two control points within a room—for example, in a bedroom at the door and at the bedside—you must choose which point you wish to dim from.

Push-button dimming

More commonly found in Europe, push-button dimmers will provide you with the same flexibility as manual dimmers, but operate slightly differently and have added benefits.

info Switches and finishes

Conventional rotary dimmers are excellent choices to maximize the flexibility of your lighting. If you need to dim from more than one point, a push-button switch (styled like a doorbell) will do this for you. A traditional "dolly," or stick switch, will simply turn lights

Slide dimmer with on/off switch

Push-button switch	Dolly switch	Rocker	Rotary dimmer	Slide dimmer

◀ ▲ Light control in action
Top left: The overhead lighting gives a dominant, practical light layer. Center left: With overhead lighting reduced, the focus is on the art, lit by directional ceiling-recessed spotlights and picture lights.

Bottom left: Floor-recessed uplights highlight architectural details. Top: Low-level lighting dominates. Dimmed picture lights and floor-based uplights are joined by ambient light from a table lamp.

The dimmer control resembles a doorbell that you depress to raise or lower the light level. This system requires an additional piece of equipment known as a remote dimmer pack. It can take much larger loads on individual circuits than can a manual dimmer and you do not need to increase the size of the unit. This system also allows you to dim from more than one control point.

on and off. There are many finishes of switch plates to complement your decorative scheme. Subtlety is key. A safe option is to match the finish of the door handles and outlet plates.

Polished chrome

Brass/antique brass

Stainless steel

Antique bronze

Nickel

Plexiglas

Painted plastic

One-room control

A one-room control system usually allows you to control four to six lighting circuits and consists of a "brain" about the size of a large paperback book, which can be installed flush into a wall. This sort of system is ideal for an open-plan room, where as many as four lighting circuits may need to be manipulated. Once wired, you can preset simple programs (or scenes) from the main unit—for example, for day, afternoon, early evening and late evening. If you have gone to the trouble and expense of designing a lighting scheme in a large space it is certainly worth installing easy-to-use controls.

Wireless systems

Wireless control is another form of control either for individual rooms or for a whole house. This type of system does not require rewiring. Usually an additional control module can be added to individual circuits—either dimmable or on/off only. For example, a specific control unit can be linked to a circuit of ceiling-recessed lights and another to the back boxes of wall lights. These modules will then communicate with a stand-alone surface-mounted control plate. You can use the control plate to manipulate individual circuits or you can set up individual scenes. This type of system is extremely useful when working in historic buildings, as it minimizes the need for new wiring.

Whole-house lighting control

If you are looking to control the lighting throughout your home, then a whole-house lighting control system is what you need. All lighting circuits in the home are wired back to a "rack." Subsidiary control plates are linked to this system, allowing you to control any lighting circuit in the house from any plate. You will need an expert to help you program your scenes on a computer. The subsidiary control plates are compact because the main rack incorporates the systems you need to manage different levels and types of loads.

Waterfall control
A lighting control system is used to manipulate the different lighting levels and separate lighting circuits inside this living room, over to the glass terrace floor beyond and to the focal point of a fiber-optic edge-lit "waterfall." An evening ambience can be created at the press of a button.

In control

A variety of control systems are available, depending on the degree of control required and the services that need to be incorporated into the system.

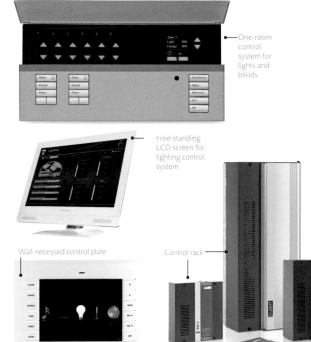

One-room control system for lights and blinds

Free-standing LCD screen for lighting control system

Control rack

Architrave plate for scene setting available in different finishes

Remote control for wireless lighting

Wall-recessed control plate

Complete home automation

If you have additional services to run, such as air conditioning, under-floor heating and audiovisual systems, then complete home automation is an efficient option. This will combine a lighting rack and additional processors and wrap up all the different controls into one control plate. This offers simple controls often from an LCD (liquid crystal display) touch screen. It also allows you remote access to all the services linked to the system, so you can turn on your lighting and air conditioning, for instance, before you arrive home.

Energy-saving controls

With complete home automation you can incorporate energy-saving controls, such as a photocell, a passive infrared detector (PIR) and/or a vacancy sensor.

■ A photocell is usually used outdoors to turn off external lights during daylight hours.
■ A PIR will switch lights on automatically when you enter a room and switch them off after a predetermined time. This is useful for small spaces such as entrances.
■ A vacancy sensor will turn lights off a predetermined amount of time after you have left a room. This is useful in children's bedrooms and playrooms, where lights might otherwise be left on.

It is worth bearing likely future developments in mind: as light sources become more energy efficient, average circuit loads are reducing dramatically. For example, a typical low-voltage spotlight provides 50 watts of light. In the future these will be replaced by 5- to 10-watt LEDs. So whatever you choose, you should ensure that it will be able to cope with the much lower loads of the future.

Making the most of what you've got

PART

2

- Harvest natural light
- Change your bulbs
- Change your shades
- Use plug-in solutions
- Introduce color

There is much you can do to improve the lighting in your home without the help of an electrician. Employ the same principles of good lighting that you would use if you were starting from scratch, and you will find that you can achieve a lot with very little effort or expenditure. Anything you can do to increase the amount of natural light in your home will be beneficial, not least because it is the most energy-efficient way to light your house. Next, review the bulbs and lamp shades that you use. Finally, consider using additional "plug-in" light fixtures to fill the gaps in your lighting scheme.

Harvest natural light

In most homes, natural light is the prime light source during the day. Making the best use of daylight is the most straightforward approach and the most eco-friendly lighting solution.

These days, most architects aim to funnel as much daylight as possible into a house. However, if you are adapting an older house, before you start to consider more complicated solutions to your lighting needs, look at the following suggestions for increasing the amount of natural light in your home or for using it to better effect.

Tips for using natural light

■ If you have small windows, remove heavy curtains and use roman blinds instead. This will allow more daylight in.

■ If privacy is an issue, consider wooden slatted blinds or louvered shutters as an alternative to net curtains. These can work even in odd-shaped windows, including large bay windows. You could also split the blinds into two segments, so that you can keep the lower levels closed for privacy and the upper levels open to let sunlight in.

■ In rooms directly under the roof, consider installing skylights and dormer windows to increase the amount of natural light. In other rooms it may be possible to increase the size of the existing windows.

■ The use of some colored glass to create a modern stained-glass window can be a stunning feature. Stained-glass windows show to maximum effect with natural light and introduce an element of color, fun, depth and texture in a room during the day.

◄ **Open house**

This hallway receives a double dose of natural light: the front door is surrounded by glass, and a sloping glass roof admits additional daylight. The overhead light can be controlled with the use of blinds. At night, square wall-mounted up/down lights enhance the architectural lines and provide a dramatic ambient light that draws the eye through the space.

◄ **Light touch**

An entire glass wall allows a maximum amount of daylight into this bedroom. Only a minimum of artificial light is needed to inject a warm, indirect background light when it gets darker in the evenings.

▲ **Roof light**

The slim slash of glass (above right) allows daylight to flow into the room below. A traditional skylight (above left) also does a great job of letting natural light in during the day. In both examples, the addition of small pin-pricks of low-voltage light in the upstands lift light levels on gloomy days and at night, making the rooms appealing to use at all times.

◀ Tall order
Sometimes all the light you need is right at your fingertips. Rather than compete with the nighttime view, a standard-voltage rope light was mounted on the underside of the central coffee table to create a soft floating effect, which helps ground the space and attract attention to the its center, rather than just to the fantastic view. This fixture is plugged into a floor socket, which makes it a great plug-in solution.

▶ Room with a view
A gentle light is inserted into the space to prevent the large expanse of glass from becoming mirrorlike at night — without detracting from the view. Separate circuits of inground uplights combine with ceiling-recessed downlights to provide flexibility and create either a practical or a more intimate light at night.

Windows at night

Wherever you decide to introduce daylight into your home, it is essential to consider the flip side. What will the room or space look and feel like at night? The key is to design artificial lighting with this in mind. Large expanses of glass at night will appear mirrorlike as you look out at the dark spaces beyond. A large area of glass also creates coldness and can be unappealing in the winter months. Here are some useful tips for countering these problems:

■ Where you have a large uncurtained window, consider what you may be able to light beyond it. Whether you overlook a yard or a roof terrace, a few strategically placed lights to uplight trees or plants will allow you to see through the glass at night, rather than simply looking at your own reflection. This also has the bonus of extending the feeling of space.

■ In skylights, the introduction of small low-voltage miniature light sources will allow you to create a soft, reflected light with an attractive twinkle. This type of treatment is especially important if you have placed your dining table under the skylight.

■ Glass lights over the top of the front door or glass panels on either side of it are classic ways to let light into the hallway during the

▼ Light beacon
The client's own hand-blown glass balls positioned on top of the cool-to-the-touch uplights create a dramatic effect from both inside and outside the space and highlight the internal texture of the glass.

day, but these options create coolness (in a visual sense) at night. As hallways are one of the most important spaces in which to create positive first impressions, it is essential to introduce a warm, welcoming light there. A lantern or pendant light in a hallway near the door will be very effective in this situation. These options have the added benefit of shedding light beyond the front door. A pair of lamps on a side table in the hallway will also add atmosphere.

Change your bulbs

You can create dramatic improvements to the lighting in your home simply by changing bulbs. It may be that you need a bulb of a higher or lower wattage or of a different shape, make or type. For example, often a large globe bulb will give a better quality of light than a standard bulb.

As part of your lighting rethink, review your choice of light sources in your home, including both standard-voltage and low-voltage bulbs. Remember that low-voltage bulbs are available in different wattages and in a variety of beam widths (see pages 22–25).

▶ **Shaded options**
The examples on the facing page show the effects of different types and wattages of bulb in dark-, medium- and light-colored shades.

With standard-voltage bulbs

Do
■ Use a frosted or pearl bulb if you can find one. They will always provide a softer, more shadow-free light and are always the best choice when the inside of a shade is a pale color or reflective.
■ Use the maximum wattage a shade will allow. You may be using a 40-watt bulb when a 60-watt bulb would instantly improve a bedside reading light.
■ Use energy-saving bulbs in your living room, kitchen and bedrooms, and save the harsh, gray-white light of fluorescent bulbs for the utility room and garage.

Don't
■ Overlight the space. Remember that, in design terms, shadow is as important as light.
■ Use a bulb of a wattage that is too great for the shade. This is especially important if you have silk shades, as these may singe or discolor and the light may cause visually distracting "hot spots."

With low-voltage bulbs

Do
■ Use a bulb of the right wattage. For example, a 20-watt/12-volt bulb is usually all that is needed to light a watercolor or line drawing. A brighter 50-watt/12-volt bulb would make the picture appear bleached out and is more appropriate for an oil painting.
■ Use a good-quality bulb. When a low-voltage spotlight is used to light artwork, this is critical for color quality. Some manufacturers make a color-constant bulb that will give true color rendition, which is essential when lighting artwork or fabrics.
■ Think about the width of beam you need for the task. If you have gone to the trouble of thinking out a lighting scheme, use a bulb with the beam width most appropriate to the task. A 40-degree beam width is a good choice for lighting a kitchen counter or for creating reflected light off a wall. A 10-degree beam width would create dramatic impact over a centerpiece on a table. A 27-degree beam provides a more generalized light but without the focus or drama.

Don't
■ Use the cheapest bulbs. These have a very short life span and poor color rendition.

40-watt/120-volt clear standard incandescent bulb

One of the most common bulbs used in households, incandescents give a warm, atmospheric glow. They also dim easily and provide a true color to the shades.

70-watt/120-volt clear energy-saving bulb (equivalent to a 100-watt standard incandescent bulb)

The energy-saving bulb is designed to reproduce similar light qualities to the standard incandescent bulb. This is a viable alternative to the traditional 100-watt bulb. This type of bulb is dimmable and provides good color to the shades.

18-watt/120-volt compact fluorescent lamp (equivalent to a 100-watt incandescent standard bulb)

Although now much improved, the light provided by compact fluorescent bulbs is flatter and grayer than that of standard or energy-saving bulbs. Although marketed as an equivalent to a 100-watt bulb, it does not appear as bright as the 70-watt energy-saving bulb.

28-watt/120-volt standard incandescent candle bulb

Commonly found in chandeliers, pendants and wall lights, the candle incandescent bulb provides a warm and dimmable light. Note how much less light is given compared to the 40-watt incandescent bulb.

25-watt/120-volt LED classic-shaped bulb equivalent to a 40-watt incandescent bulb

This demonstrates the best type of LED bulb available at present. Note that most of the light travels upward, with very little downward spill.

Change your shades

Shades hide the bulb and diffuse the intensity of the light emitted. The range of materials used is vast, and the variety of styles is equally huge. But always remember to choose a shade for what it will do for the light in a room, and not just for how pleasing it looks.

Table and floor lamps provide essential building blocks for light in a room. If you can light a room only by table and floor lamps, it makes the choice of shade even more important. You need to maximize the light available and also ensure that you get the light where you want it. Because your eye is always drawn to the brightest point in a space, shades can be the first thing to make a visual impact in a room. You can improve the lighting and update the look and feel of any room by reviewing the shades. The shape, size, material, color and lining are all key to a shade's look and use. For the lighting designer, the key is to choose a shade that not only complements the decor but, more importantly, directs the light in the way you intend.

▲ Square symmetry
Square, tapered shades add a modern twist to traditional crystal lamp bases and sit comfortably within a classically styled room. The width of the base of the shades allows large pools of light to spill onto the table.

▼ Size matters
A small lamp used in an open-plan space is easily lost and creates a fussy rather than elegant look.

▲ Eye holes

Experiment with the different effects a variety of shade shapes and materials can bring. This punched design is layered to hide any direct light source. A soft, diffused light edges its way through the layers to make an eye-catching centerpiece.

▼ Hall solution

An eye-shaped shade (a flattened oval shape) is an elegant solution for tight spaces. The white lining of the gold shade and the height of the base allow plenty of light to escape, both up and down.

Tips for choosing shades

■ Light-colored shades in silk, parchment and paper will cast a relatively cool light as the bulb transmits the color of the shade.
■ A cream-colored silk-pleated coolie-style shade is a safe option but is often a poor choice, as it does not effectively shade the light source or add anything to a room.
■ For a moody, atmospheric glow, go for dark colors such as chocolate and deep purple.
■ A lined shade will mellow the light source. Unlined shades tend to allow a hot spot of light to show through the shade. This can be distracting, as the eye is always drawn to the brightest point. As a quick fix, you can spray paint the inside of the shade gold to give a warm glow to the room.

■ Don't be afraid to experiment with unexpected combinations. For example, a black shade with a lime-green lining can look fresh and perky, or a red lining (right) can give a moody, low-key light.
■ Always opt for fewer lamps with larger shades.

Shaded bulb

Classic oval

Metallic round

Shade shape and size

Coolie (or Empire) The most common shape of shade, a sloped coolie shade pushes most of the light downward, giving confined pools of light. Because of this, only the largest of these shades produce useful amounts of light. Much can be done to improve the levels of light in a room by changing shades of this shape.

Drum A drum-shaped (deep or shallow) shade allows light to escape both upward and downward, adding to the ambient light but also giving task light below. Also, this is a good shape for showing off the fabric from which the shade is made.

Oval The deep or slim oval performs in a similar way to a drum shape, but can be a better choice if you have less space.

Eye shape The contemporary "eye-shaped" shade (eye shaped as seen from above) is a sophisticated design. It allows light to escape both upward and downward but in narrow pools, and it, therefore, is not the best choice if you have only a few lamps and need a lot of light. However, this shape is a great choice for a lamp on a narrow console table in a hallway.

Cylinder This elegant shape provides a contemporary feel on a candlestick-style lamp.

Conical Typically found on small candlestick lamps, this shape of shade is suitable for narrow pockets of light. Even in a large size, the shape pushes most of the light downward.

Square and tapered square A square shade instantly updates a room. It gives great light both upward and downward and is often useful in a corner. The tapered square is a sleek shape to use on a traditional swing-arm bedside reading light and will give more useful light than a conical shade.

Rectangle and tapering rectangle Much like the square shape, rectangular shades provide a refreshing and modern look. Shades of this shape are often useful on a bar or side table.

Material effect
A black shade (top) forces all of its light down. A medium-toned shade (center) provides a welcoming glow. A metal-ringed shade (bottom) casts dramatic reflections.

info Shade shapes, sizes and finishes

It really is worth experimenting to see the difference the shape and size of the shade can make. The size needs to be appropriate to the task and to the height of the base. When making your selection, bear in mind that the more open the shape, the more light will escape. A number of shades are illustrated in profile, with an icon indicating their interior shape. Choose a finish that helps to soften or lift light levels, depending on what you need to achieve.

Tip

Use a small number of large table- or floor-based lamps and shades rather than many smaller ones. With a larger size you will get a better light and the impression of less clutter, which in turn makes a room feel more spacious.

Perfect balance

Two large classic table lamps with wide-necked, gently sloped shades cast sufficient light both upward and downward to provide a warm atmosphere, without the addition of other table lamps. The color of the shades ensures the bulb cannot be seen.

Squat coolie

Traditional coolie

Large coolie

Traditional pagoda

Standard circular

Ornate mini shade

Contemporary pagoda

Contemporary rectangle

Square

Shaved rectangle

Contemporary drum

Oval

Use plug-in solutions

A plug-in light source is any form of movable light or lamp—from a floor-based low-voltage highlighter to a linear light strip—that is plugged into a socket rather than permanently wired into your domestic power supply. These instant lighting solutions can radically change the ambience of a room.

Positioned judiciously, a plug-in solution will add instant drama. Use this type of light in the dead corners of rooms to highlight and enlarge the space, behind large plants to create fantastic patterns of shadow and light on a wall, or behind a plinth for a dramatic backlight to an object of interest. The great thing about a portable light source is that you can play with various effects and positions and move the light around the room to suit your changing needs or moods.

Lighting corners and objects

A dark corner or a lack of focus in a room can be addressed by introducing a small floor-standing uplight. The best type of lamp for this purpose is a low-voltage version. This will allow you to control the beam width you use. For example, a wide beam is suited to uplighting behind a plant in a corner. This creates natural shape and shadow as the light travels through the leaves. Equally, a pair of floor-based uplights fitted with narrow-beam bulbs will uplight a fireplace to create an instant focal point.

Positioned on a mantel or table, a low-voltage tabletop spotlight can be used to draw attention to a painting, sculpture or other objet d'art. Objects such as vases can also be backlit by a plug-in linear light source, such as a strip of low-voltage capsule lamps.

▶ **Discreet design**
A miniature low-voltage tabletop spotlight focuses attention on objects on display where no other light source is available.

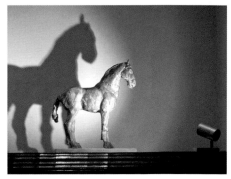

▲ **Clear visibility**
The flexibility offered by a plug-in solution can often produce a better result for the object being lit than that provided by a fixed source. A low-voltage fixture (pictured here) is the preferred choice for lighting works of art because it provides the best color rendition.

◀ **Iconic balance**
A plug-in light source can add a touch of class to a room. The iconic Arco floor light, with its perfect balance between its heavy marble base and contemporary shade, provides a stylish boost to levels of lighting in any interior.

▶ **Minimalist discretion**
A discreet low-voltage plug-in floor-based uplight adds depth to this space, highlighting the beautifully curved arm of the sofa and reflecting in the mirror hung above.

▼ **Perfect pair**
A simple pair of candlestick lamps on the narrow console provide a welcoming light in this hallway and draw the eye to the artwork.

Plug-in control

It is best to use plug-in lights on a specific (5-amp) lighting circuit. This will allow you to control your light on a dimmer from a single point. If this is not possible, try to have an in-line dimmer fitted to give you more flexibility.

A low-voltage floor-based uplight is a useful and flexible tool for adding dramatic touches to any room. It is compact so can be positioned in tight spaces.

Introduce color

An instant and reversible solution to a dull lighting scheme that will certainly create impact is color. However, don't go overboard with color effects; for a sophisticated look, opt for delicate hues rather than bold primaries.

If you already have 50-watt/12-volt spotlights, you can replace them with colored versions in deep magenta, blue, green or yellow for an instant color effect. Even more cheaply, a colored gel sheet, widely available from art suppliers, can be cut to fit temporarily over an existing uplight for a fun party atmosphere. This will also allow you to see the effects of introducing color without making a big investment. Never leave a temporary gel on a hot fixture for more than a few hours—they can melt. Fluorescent tubes are another means of creating an instant change of scene. Because they emit little heat, these are often more suitable—that is, safer—for placing behind curtains or on top of units. Colored gel sleeves to slip over tubes are available in a wide variety of colors.

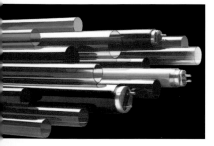

◀ **Gel sleeves**
A simple way of achieving an intriguing range of color effects, the simplicity of a gel sleeve that simply slides over a fluorescent tube is hard to beat.

◀ **Colored backdrop**
Provide impact with fluorescent tubes placed behind a gel sheet to back a screen. The colour and screen create a dramatic play of shadows.

▲ **Mind bending**
Color can quickly change the perception of a space and can alter a mood instantly. Evenly spaced fluorescent tubes covered with colored gel sleeves provide an easy and economic way to inject a dense, saturated color into a space. The pink invites you into the space, while the blue creates a cooler, more restrained, mood.

Light contrast
A sleeved fluorescent tube adds a magenta glow behind the peacock-blue curtains, providing a neat counterpoint to the colored-glass lamp base and purple headboard, lifting an area that might otherwise be a dead space.

Introducing color

- A sheet of colored gel can be cut to fit an uplight to provide a temporary lift of color for a party.
- Colored 12-volt bulbs and LED bulbs for table lamps can offer a more permanent saturation of color.
- Gel sleeves that slide over fluorescent batons come in a rainbow of colors for a safe and economical injection of color.

Add a dimmer

If you do nothing else, give yourself the flexibility to dim your plug-in lights, to give an instant change of mood. There are many products available that allow you to add a dimmer to any plug-in fixture without the need for an electrician. Dimmers plug into the power outlet of your lamp and offer you the option of dimming your light source locally.

3

Principles of good lighting

- Fixed recessed downlights
- Recessed directional spotlights
- Surface-mounted lighting
- Track lighting
- Cable systems
- Wall-mounted uplighting and downlighting
- Floor-recessed uplights and wall-recessed floor washers
- Concealed lighting
- Cove and coffer lighting
- Slot and niche lighting
- Mirror lighting
- Task lighting
- Special effects lighting

Good lighting is all about choosing what you need to light, choosing the right "tools"—the fixtures—for the job and positioning those fixtures effectively. Do not be afraid to break from the standard neat and tidy "grid" of lights in the ceiling. This may look satisfyingly ordered on a plan but will do nothing to enhance your space. Think about what the light is doing in the room and learn to "paint" with light. You should consider using both architectural lighting and decorative pieces when assembling a lighting scheme. Architectural light is lighting that is built into the fabric of the building or structures within the space, and this kind of lighting should be subtle and unseen. The more discreet it is, the more effective it will be. Decorative lighting is clearly meant to be seen and should enhance the visual richness of the room.

Fixed recessed downlights

Positioned wisely, a fixed or static low-voltage downlight can "lift" a space and is a simple way to provide valuable additional light to an interior.

▶ Dramatic repetition
A row of downlights is positioned to skim light down the surface of this storage unit. The simplicity of the effect creates a dramatic result. Good-quality bulbs are used to achieve accurate color rendition.

A low-glare downlight will highlight the focal point in a room while not becoming the focal point itself. A good-quality downlight is designed to allow the bulb to sit deeply within the fixture to prevent glare. Remember, however, that the quality of the bulb you use is more important than the shape of the fixture (see Choosing a Light Source, pages 22–25). Standard voltage downlights will not provide you with the same crisp white light as a low-voltage downlight. They run much hotter and do not have the same beam-width capacity as a low-voltage bulb. Be sure to select the appropriate beam width to achieve the desired effect (see Beam Widths at right).

Use a downlight to achieve
■ A practical level of light in a room—for example, in a playroom, utility room, kitchen or hallway.
■ A dramatic accent—for example, over a dining table, for a sculpture or onto a coffee table.
■ A crisp light to enhance floor color and texture—for example, in a hallway.
■ A skim of light down a textured surface, door or niche.
■ Good color rendition, allowing you to distinguish colors of furnishings or artworks accurately.

■ HARDWARE

A thin bezel and a bulb that is set deep within the fixture will always give the best low-glare light to the space, whichever beam width you choose. A fixed ceiling ring, rather than a curly spring, will ensure the bulb is easy to change.

BEAM WIDTHS

1 Fixed recessed downlights are available in beam widths between zero and 60 degrees.
2 They can be set very close to a wall to pick out texture.
3 Lights can be used to create a pool of light on the floor.

◀ Firehood
When a hole is made in a ceiling to accommodate a recessed downlight, it is a good idea to install a firehood to maintain fire safety.

| Round downlight, deep baffle | Waterproof downlight | Capsule light with reflective backplate | Square downlight in a fixed position |

1 Point of interest

A downlight positioned directly over an object will cast strong light on top of the object and natural shadows under the object being lit. This is a useful way to highlight sculptures and create strong focal points.

2 Background wash

LED downlights set close to the wall wash down the cabinet doors to highlight the panels and provide reflected light, which is more flattering than a direct overhead light.

3 Textured tiles

Downlights skim light down this tiled surface in a small shower room to highlight its texture. This draws the eye to the farthest point and expands the sense of space.

4 Niche point

A single LED downlight is set within a niche. The strength of the light source is contained within the recess to provide strong reflected light to the object displayed. Illuminated niches are a useful way to introduce light at a different level to that of the ceiling.

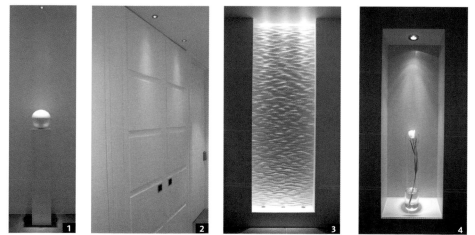

■ FINISHES

A white finish on spotlights is usually unobtrusive. However, colored or metal finishes work well in natural woods, especially dark woods. If you have a colored ceiling, get the fixtures professionally sprayed to match.

| White/Black | Brushed steel | Nickel | Chrome | Bronze | Brass |

Planning your downlighting scheme

Having understood the theory of how to manipulate a fixed downlight, you can consider how to use it in your own home to best effect. First decide what it is that you want to light and choose the best beam width for the task. Next, plan the most suitable position for the fixture. Finally, select the style and finish of the downlight fixture.

Styles of downlight fixture

Downlight fixtures can be either round, square or oblong. Remember that the bulb will always be round. The classic option is the round fixture. However, a square or oblong fixture works well in modern spaces where clean lines predominate. Occasionally a mix of round and square/oblong fixtures can also work well—for example, in a kitchen where an island can be lit with oblong downlights and the cabinets with round directional fixtures.

The housings of downlights are available in a number of different finishes, which you can choose to match to the room. For use in ceilings choose a fixture that blends with the surrounding color. A metal finish on the bezel (the outer edge of the fixture), such as stainless steel, polished chrome or nickel, is best suited for use within joinery details or tiling, such as in shelves and bathroom niches.

Mosaic sparkle
Sealed downlights set close to the back wall skim light down iridescent mosaic tiles to create sparkle. This treatment enhances the depth and, thus, the sense of space in the shower.

BEAM WIDTHS IN DOWNLIGHTS

Low-voltage bulbs are available in various beam widths. Using these to best effect makes a big difference to your lighting scheme and the objects to be lit. This is especially true when lighting artwork. Notice the intensity and spread of beam cast on the fireplace shelf.

10° beam width The narrowest beam is the best to use to create dramatic pools of light to illuminate single objects over dining tables or in narrow slot niches.

15° beam width A tight beam (but not too tight) is useful for lighting smaller artworks and for creating a pool of light over a coffee table, for example.

Beam mix
Medium-beam bulbs are used to light the closet doors in this playroom and provide adequate reflected light into the play area. Narrow-beam bulbs cross-light the ship.

info Louvers and lenses

Louvers and lenses can be used to soften or eliminate the hard edges of an arc of light that occur, for example, where a line of recessed downlights is used to skim light down a wall. Softening lenses will soften the light output, and a sandblasted lens will eliminate the hard edges entirely.

Sandblasted lens

Lenses should also be employed when lighting artwork to create a more focused light in the center of the piece and remove arcs and hot spots. Only strong oil paintings light well without a lens; a watercolor needs a delicate light that has been subdued with a sandblasted lens. Every piece of art is different, so it is worth experimenting with different beam widths and lenses to get the best result.

Softening lens

Linear-spread lens

A honeycomb fitting placed in front of the bulb will remove around 30 percent of the light output for a softer light, which is useful at entrances and exits of rooms. Always check if lenses can be used in your chosen fixture as not all ceiling-recessed fixtures are designed to take them.

Honeycomb fitting

With valuable paintings and delicate fabrics, it is worth inserting an ultraviolet filtering lens into the fixture, which will cut out a large percentage of the damaging rays.

27° beam width A medium beam width works well for washing light down a vertical surface, such as a kitchen or wardrobe unit, or to light art.

40° or 55° beam width A wide wash of light is most suitable when a very general spread of light is needed—for example, in playrooms or utility rooms.

Do

■ Use downlights sparingly, only where light is needed.
■ Choose from the variety of beam widths available—for example, a wide beam for infill lighting and a narrow beam for accents.
■ Mix downlighting with a different level of light, such as that provided by table lamps or uplights, to add the impression of texture to a space.
■ Use a good-quality bulb designed for long life and accurate color rendition.
■ Use lenses and louvers to soften scallops (see page 67).

Don't

■ Install downlights in a grid pattern or even formation in the ceiling. This will light only the floor and diminish the sense of space.
■ Use downlights with a shallow baffle. This will create glare and draw the eye to the light instead of to the object or area being lit.
■ Choose fixed downlights to light wall-hung artwork. Use directional downlights instead (see pages 70–75).

▲ Niche highlights
Downlights highlight the objects in the niches to draw the eye through the space and provide reflected light. This allows for less light to be used in the ceiling.

▶ Dramatic scallops
A row of downlights, positioned closely to the wall headboard, wash light down the wall. The light from the narrow-beam bulbs without lenses creates an interesting scalloped pattern.

Recessed directional spotlights

Increasing the amount of reflected light in a space is the key to good lighting, and, used properly, the recessed directional spotlight will do just this. Making the most of reflected light is a great way to reduce the number of fixtures you need. The directional spotlight is also best for lighting artwork.

The exciting thing about using a directional spotlight to provide reflected light instead of relying on a straight downlight is that it can fulfill a number of tasks in your lighting scheme. A directional light bounces light off a straight plane or wall and back into the space. This is by far the most subtle way to light a room. You can also use this type of light source to pick out features, such as a picture or a sculpture, at the same time. This method for providing adequate light to a space is more thoughtful than spattering the ceiling with recessed downlights.

Choosing a fixture

The more expensive spotlight fixtures tend to have a deeper baffle (that is, the place where the bulb is set back within the fixture) than the cheaper equivalents. It is also worth searching out a fixture with a black inner baffle rather than a white one. A black baffle will help to reduce glare further.

As with straight downlights, the directional downlight does not have to be round. Square and oblong versions as well as multiple units (where there is more than one light within a fixture) are also available. The round fixture is the classic shape and easily blends into the background surface. More care needs to be taken using square and

BEAM WIDTHS IN DIRECTIONAL SPOTS

1. 55° beam width
Creates a wide beam suitable for general wall washes or to light very large pictures for which several fixtures might be needed.

2. 40° beam width
Useful for reflecting general light into a space and for lighting a single large picture.

3. 27° beam width
Use to light small or medium-sized pictures.

4. 15° beam width
Will provide a focused light on sculptures and works of art.

5. 10° beam width
Use this narrow beam to light small paintings or to spotlight a small sculpture.

■ DIRECTIONAL FIXTURES

Look for a fixture with a slim bezel and a deep baffle. Also check the degree of tilt. Most fixtures provide 30 degrees, but a greater degree of tilt will offer more flexibility. A fixed ceiling ring rather than a curly spring will ensure bulbs are easier to change.

Round directional spotlight | Square directional spotlight | LED directional spotlight

◀ Light work
A pair of ceiling-recessed spotlights, with 15-degree beam-width bulbs, cross-light the artwork to create a strong point of interest on a landing. Reflected light spills onto the stylish chair, providing an additional focus.

oblong fixtures, as these can be visually distracting unless set out evenly, which may defeat the purpose of using directional lights. The latter two types sit most comfortably within a contemporary space.

Any transformer fitted should be of good quality. This is an essential piece of equipment, and it is worth paying attention to it. It may not seem as important as the fixture itself, but a good transformer can extend the life span of the bulbs and provide more efficient dimming.

Bulbs for spotlights

Always choose a good-quality bulb. Some manufacturers make specific bulbs for the very best color rendering. These are known as color-constant bulbs. Use this type of

▲ Directional wash
In this bedroom, directional spotlights are used to wash light down the front of the closets. The ceiling detail meant it was not possible to get light fixtures close to the doors, so directional spots with a 36-degree tilt were used to light the doors and provide reflected light to the space.

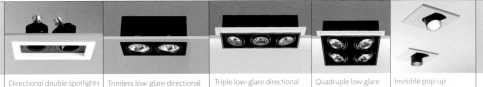

| Directional double spotlights with trim | Trimless low-glare directional double spotlights | Triple low-glare directional spotlights with trim | Quadruple low-glare directional spotlights | Invisible pop-up recessed spotlight |

Do

■ Use directional spotlights sparingly, only fit them where light is needed.

■ Choose a fixture with a deep baffle for lowglare and unobtrusive light.

■ Check the degree of tilt on the fixture. A tilt of 35 degrees or more will provide you with flexibility.

■ Select the focal points—for example, artworks—that you want to light.

■ Ensure that the fixture is positioned correctly. The correct position for an adjustable directional fixture will depend on the height of the ceiling, the degree of tilt of the fixture and the exact position of the object to be lit.

■ Use an appropriate lens to achieve the best effect and a soft, even light (see page 67).

Don't

■ Use more fixtures than you need. It is a waste of energy, and you will reduce the impact of the lighting.

■ Use fixtures without a baffle, or you risk creating glare to which the eye will be drawn, instead of drawing it to the object you intend to light.

■ Position directional lights in a sloping ceiling. Only rarely will the angle of the fixture lend itself to giving a subtle light.

Constant focus
Directional ceiling-recessed spots provide a gentle wide wash of light down the front of this display unit to pick out the color and texture of the objects on display. This is a flexible way to light collections of objects, allowing you to move or change the items without disrupting the lighting scheme.

bulb (available in various beam widths) when lighting art or when lighting curtained areas. This should ensure that your gold silk curtains really do look gold (not green) and that your painting is seen as the artist intended.

Use directional spotlights to provide
■ Reflected light in a space.
■ The most effective lighting for artwork.
■ Strong focal points in a room.

Positioning the fixtures
A ceiling-recessed spotlight should emphasize the object or space that it lights and not become the focus of attention itself. When you start to plan the locations of the recessed spotlights in your lighting scheme, you need to consider the precise effect you want to achieve. It is best to keep the style of the fixture simple for an understated result. As with the recessed downlight, a neutral-colored bezel for a fixture is suitably discreet. Save chrome or matte black finishes for special applications, such as recessing in natural wood shelving units.

Flexible lighting
A multidirectional spotlight creates a flexible lighting plan. This type of spotlight, set in the ceiling on the far left and far right, is used here to highlight the grain of the wood of the cabinets (inset), but it could also be used to highlight objects on the console table or sofa.

Using lenses

A low-voltage spotlight will produce round pools of light, creating circles or arcs of light on the wall. This effect can be reduced by inserting a lens into the fixture in front of the bulb, which "smoothes" away the striations and arcs to leave a softer, less obvious light. Various lenses are available to create different effects. A sandblasted lens (or heavily frosted disk of glass) gives a very subtle wash of light on a wall. A softening lens does the same thing but allows more light to get through, and a spreader lens helps squeeze the light through a vertical or horizontal axis, depending on how it is positioned within the fixture. (See also Louvers and Lenses, page 67).

Lighting artwork

It is important to choose a strength of light to suit the object to be lit. Not every picture requires a typical 50-watt/12-volt light—for example, a watercolor can be lit to best effect with a 20-watt or 35-watt bulb, while an oil painting in strong colors may benefit from a 50-watt light. There are no hard and fast rules when lighting art. The best way to achieve the most effective light is to experiment with bulb strengths, beam widths and lenses.

Using a framing projector

The most dramatic way of using recessed directional light to light artwork is to use a framing projector. This piece of equipment directs the light through a "cut-out" or "template" that exactly matches the shape of the object to be lit. The light therefore "frames" the object (artwork or sculpture) perfectly. The result is worth the investment for a truly special work of art.

Framing projectors are concealed in a recess in the ceiling (you will need a void at least 55 inches (140 cm) deep and an access trap, preferably in the ceiling) or in bookcases or, in some cases, in the floor. You will need a lighting designer to help you make the most of this option and an expert installer to cut the template to match the object to be lit exactly.

Lighting a mirror

Directional spotlights are also a great way to light mirrors. Just as mirrors reflect natural light from a window, they will provide added sparkle when lit with a narrow-beam spot. Even old-style antique mirrors can benefit from this lighting treatment. A correctly positioned directional spot

Soft silks
Directional spots with softening lenses wash light down the curtain treatments to ensure the window bay does not become lost at night and to highlight the curtains. Softening lenses soften any hard arcs and hot spots of light on the fabric.

Textured highlight
An accurately positioned medium-beam directional spotlight provides good light to the mirror and the face of whoever will be using it, and also brings the texture of the pebble wall to life.

lighting a mirror over a vanity provides fantastically clear light to the face. Any harshness and unwanted shadows can be easily rectified by the addition of some warm side lighting (see Mirror Lighting, pages 118–123).

Spotlighting window areas

You can use a directional spotlight to wash light down fabric blinds, shutters or curtains. This increases the sense of daylight in the room during the day (useful on days when the light is flat, overcast and dull) and highlights the color and texture of the fabric. What is more, when curtains and blinds are drawn at night, this added light prevents "dead spots" in the room.

The same technique can be applied to lighting shelving. If it is not possible to install recessed light sources, lighting these areas from above will draw attention to ornaments and books. In a bedroom or dressing room, you can also use directional spots to wash light onto the front of a closet unit to give an even reflected light in the room as well as providing light into the unit when open.

LEDs for spots

LED replacements for both standard-voltage and low-voltage bulbs are now more readily available. However, the output and color rendition are not yet as good as that of the bulbs they replace.

Surface-mounted lighting

Where no recess space is available or where it is not practical to position lights in a ceiling void, a surface-mounted fixture will provide a similar effect to a recessed fixture. This type of fixture can also be used to light artwork and to punch light upward to highlight architectural details.

Surface-mounted fixtures come in many shapes and sizes. They can be designed as spotlights (with integral or remote transformers) or as a fixture specifically designed to uplight. Both types of fixture are obviously more visible than a recessed version, so it is important to position them with care to ensure that both the light source itself and the fixture are as discreet as possible.

Surface-mounted spotlights

These can generally be used with standard voltage, low-voltage dichroic or capsule bulbs. You will always get a better result with a low-voltage version, as you have more control over the beam width and a better quality of color rendition. This type of fixture can be ceiling mounted or fixed to joists or cross timbers.

Seek out a design that has the bulb tucked up into the fixture or use a fixture that has a glare cowl to reduce light spill and ensure the concentration of light is directed where you want it. Many fixtures will take lenses and louvers to help soften and shape the light in the same way as a recessed directional spot.

A surface-mounted spotlight can wash a wall with light when it houses a capsule lamp. This type of light source can also be used to light a large feature on wall, such as a tapestry or work of art.

HOW TO USE

Directional surface-mounted spotlight
Use a surface-mounted directional spotlight to light artwork or to wash light onto walls. Choose a fixture to which you can add lenses for a softer effect.

Surface-mounted spotlight as a downlight
This enables you to wash light down bathroom or shower walls when there is no recess. Use several in a row for a stronger effect. Vary the beam widths to create strong patterns of light.

Surface-mounted up- and downlights
Use a narrow-beam bulb in a surface-mounted spotlight to highlight architectural details. Mount the fixtures on the sides of beams or on walls.

■ SURFACE-MOUNTED FIXTURES

Choose function over style when selecting a surface-mounted fixture. It does not matter how good a fixture looks if it can't light what you need it to. Finish is also important. Select a finish that blends with the surface on which it is mounted. It is worth remembering that an aluminum fixture can work even in traditional settings, as any light will reflect off it so that it blends with its surroundings.

Spotlight with deep baffle | Low-glare spotlight | Wall washer

◄ Clean infill
Surface-mounted
spotlights are set on
the upstand of the
ceiling to provide
general light to the
hallway.

▲ Light and space
In a shower where no recess
is available, a pair of surface-
mounted downlights provide
a restful and practical light,
highlighting the color and
texture of the tiles (top). Above,
a traditional fixture skims
dramatic light down metro-style
tiles. The use of a wide-beam
bulb provides an eye-catching
feature and draws the eye
to the back of the shower,
expanding the sense of space.

Fixed tubular downlight

Tubular twin spotlight

Adjustable tubular
spotlight

Glare cowl

Paired layers

A general wash of uplight is achieved using surface-mounted uplights set on top of the beams. They highlight the structural detail and open out the space in this corridor. Surface-mounted spotlights are positioned on top of the beams to light the paintings and sculpture.

When using a low-voltage spotlight, it is essential to consider the location of the transformer. This can be remote or electronic and will be a limiting factor in the location of the fixture. An electronic transformer will usually have to be placed within 3 feet (1 m) of the fixture, whereas a remote one can be positioned up to 13 feet (4 m) away or farther, depending on the type chosen and the width of cable used. If this is not possible, choose a fixture with an integral transformer.

Surface-mounted uplights

Domestic-supply voltage incandescent uplights can sit in a purpose-built housing and be positioned on top of beams to uplight a void—for example, in an A-frame-style roof. This type of lighting is easy to install and will give a bright, reflected light that can be mellowed by a dimmer. However, these lights do get hot and, therefore, must be positioned with care. It is often best to sit such fixtures on top of a heat-resistant plinth. Energy-saving alternatives such as IRC incandescent bulbs (see page 26) are now available, but as energy efficiency becomes more

▲ Style statement
Architectural-style tube fixtures house low-voltage dichoric bulbs, which are ideal for lighting art. The jointed design also allows these fixtures to provide infill light where needed. Here the lights make a visual impact that is as strong as that of the paintings.

◄ Delicate touch
A delicate effect is achieved using a discreetly positioned surface-mounted low-voltage spotlight to highlight the front of a drinks' cabinet. The low-voltage light helps to enhance the sparkle of the bottles and glassware within.

Do

■ Use in a subtle way. Where possible, position the fixture out of sight.
■ Consider maintenance. Can you always get to the fixture relatively easily to change a bulb?
■ Always consider where a transformer (remote or electronic) or driver will be located.

Don't

■ Be tempted to use a surface-mounted fixture where the ceiling is low (below 7½ feet (2.3 m)). It will crowd the room and make the ceiling look even lower.
■ Use hot light sources such as incandescent halogen lamps without considering the surrounding material on which the fixture is positioned.

important and technology moves on, this type of lighting is being superseded by energy-saving sources with lower heat output, such as linear LED.

Use a surface-mounted fixture to achieve

■ A practical but discreet level of light in a room when no recess void is available.
■ Good light for works of art.
■ A general wash over walls or an uplight into a roof.

Surface-mounted lighting in practice

These key tips will help you to avoid the common pitfalls involved with the installation of surface-mounted lighting.
■ Fitted to a flat ceiling and positioned at the correct distance away from the piece, a surface-mounted spotlight will light a work of art. However, this will be a very visible solution. A design that has a knuckle joint to allow the fixture to tilt and twist will allow more flexibility for positioning the fixture out of sight.
■ When a table is positioned below a skylight, a low-glare surface spotlight can be mounted on the upstand of the skylight to direct light down onto the table and provide a practical level of light when needed and a more subtle glow when dimmed, for example, for late-night dining. This works equally well where a sloping glass roof has been used to extend a space in a kitchen, for example.
■ In old barn conversions and contemporary loft conversions, both surface-mounted spotlights and surface-mounted uplights can be used to highlight architectural details. A surface-mounted spot can be fitted to the side of a beam to direct light to the center of the room or over a coffee table, for example.
■ Fixed (non-adjustable) surface-mounted spots can also be used to skim light down walls. This is useful in a bathroom or shower with no recess, where using a suitably watertight fixture mounted above eye level will skim light down tiles or a wall. This can look dramatic as well as provide functional light.

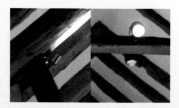

◄► The big picture
Surface-mounted spotlights bring this almost triple-height space alive by inserting light into the highest points to illuminate the historic structure and open out the space. A low-glare surface-mounted spotlight skims light up (far left), and a pair of 100-watt fixtures pool light onto the table below and light the picture on the chimney (left and opposite).

Track lighting

A well-designed track light provides a flexible solution where no recess depth is available to light artworks or when you need general lighting on a limited budget.

This type of lighting is an easy-to-install and, often, economic solution. However, it is worth remembering that most types of track lighting offer poor glare control. The most popular design is a cluster on a single surface-mounted plate, which is not a good choice for general lighting, providing only scattered beams of light. In such cases it is often more effective to install a pendant.

Choosing the right track

If track lighting is the only or the preferred option, it is wise to invest in a good-quality low-voltage version. Steer clear of the standard cluster design, and instead opt for a linear version, which will be less busy on a ceiling and less likely to draw the eye. Occasionally a particular pattern of track can work well—for example, a complete circle of surface-mounted track over a round kitchen island. The most important thing is to identify where the light is required and, therefore, what shape of track would be most suitable. The most successful installations are those in which the track does not make its own statement.

A low-voltage track system allows you the advantage of using good-quality bulbs with a precise beam width that will provide the best light. You will also be able to use clip-on lenses or honeycomb louvers to create soft light. You will always need to consider the location of the

TRACK OPTIONS

Straight track
A linear track system that allows lighting to be angled to either side will always look better than a cluster of spots.

Twin-rail track
A more decorative version of the straight track, a twin-rail system in which both light sources can be used side by side with spotlights offers more flexibility than a single track.

Picture light track
A linear system which can be fixed directly to the wall or ceiling, which uses a stalk-style spotlight—useful for lighting art.

■ TRACK FIXTURES

A simple-looking system will always work well. If possible, choose a fixture where the bulb is set deep into it to minimize glare, and choose a system that you can accessorize with cowls to shield the bulbs.

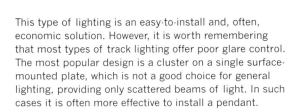

| Simple track-mounted spot | Set down track spot | White set down track spot | Minimal backed lamp spot | Retro styled track spot |

◄ Surface solution

A track system is often used to provide light to multiple surfaces where no recess is available. The fixtures are designed to ensure the bulbs cannot be seen from any angle.

◄ Flexible twin

A twin-rail system allows for the addition of more decorative fixtures to a scheme. Spotlights provide the more practical light, while a shaded downlight pools a softer light in the center of the space.

▲ Playful curves

Curves can be a great way to introduce an element of fun into a playroom or children's bedroom. Beware of creating too many curves, as it is not the fixture that should be the focal point but the object being lit.

transformer for a low-voltage track. Some track systems incorporate a transformer mounted on the surface of the track. While this keeps everything compact and makes for easier installation, these types of transformers are not always dimmable. If possible, opt for a dimmable version. Remote transformers are often used, but designs that can be wall mounted are also available. Where possible, choose a remote transformer that can be hidden.

Track mount spot on arm

Recessed track with stalk spots

Adaptable recessed track

Anti-glare louvers on spots

Adaptable non-recessed track

An LED light source can be used in a track system. However, the light output is relatively weak—the best are comparable to approximately 20-watt/12-volt output, and the light tends to be dull and gray. Miniature fiber-optic track systems can be an inconspicuous option when you need to light delicate objects in a display cabinet.

A useful tip to bear in mind is that the track does not necessarily have to be surface-mounted to the ceiling. Some systems can be suspended from anything that can hang (either on a wire or a fixed rod), making the whole fixture less obtrusive.

Displaying works of art

Track lighting provides the ability to shift the positions of light sources and to group fixtures to light specific objects or areas. A remote-controlled track light system allows you to adjust both the positions and the angle of tilt of the fixtures to achieve the best result without the use of a ladder, which makes this task much easier. This makes track lighting a great choice where works of art or other objects of interest are changed on a regular basis.

In small spaces

Narrow spaces where no recess is available—for example, galley kitchens—often benefit from track-mounted

Do

- Use a low-voltage version for sharp, bright light.
- Choose low-voltage track when flexibility is required, such as to light works of art that are changed frequently.
- Fit clip-on lenses and louvers to prevent glare when fixtures are not ideally positioned.
- Try to choose a dimmable version to provide greater flexibility.
- Use silver-backed bulbs to prevent a pink back-glow.

Don't

- Choose standard-voltage spotlights when other options are available.
- Use cluster spots, as these are prime sources of glare.
- Select a non-dimmable version.

Punchy spotlights
A very large painting will often benefit from punchy spotlights. Oils in particular respond well to being lit with low voltage. The deep cowls prevent glare.

◄ **Concrete solution**
A simple track system provides a budget-friendly solution where a concrete ceiling does not allow for any recesses. The adjustability of the spots makes it easy to aim the light where it is most needed.

▼ **Miniature mounts**
A miniature vertical track can provide ideal localised pools of specific light to artwork. These LED spots are a cool, safe option for lighting valuable works of art.

spotlights, which can be directed either side of the room to provide effective light to the walls and work surfaces.

Within cabinets

A collection of objects in a display cabinet can be effectively and safely lit by a miniature track system. In these situations it is best to employ a fiber-optic kit, which avoids the risk of overheating. The color can easily be adjusted by using gel sheets. An alternative to fiber optics is a dichroic bulb fixture, although this will create heat and the color rendition and bulb life will not be as good.

Cable systems

A contemporary and understated way to light a space where no ceiling fixing is available, a cable system is a highly flexible option.

A cable system provides more options than a fixed-track system. Most systems allow you the choice of low-voltage bulb strengths (50, 75 and even 100 watts). For this reason, it is an ideal solution for rooms with high ceilings or where no recess space is available. The choice of a 100-watt low-voltage bulb will provide a certain amount of general light from ceilings as high as 12 feet (3.5m).

Most systems have a variety of lamp designs from which to choose. The best looking are often semi-industrial and minimal. The aim is to ensure the system "floats" in the space to provide a seemingly effortless light source.

In track systems, the fixtures are often fixed in place and limit the areas you can light. With a cable system, you can move the lamps (or fixtures) along the wire to where the light is required. With some fixtures the angle of the lamp can easily be swiveled through 180 degrees and will therefore provide uplight as well as angled downlight. Use a wide-beam low-glare bulb to give good downlight onto a workspace, and angle a narrow-beam

Simply strectched
The minimalism of the fully adjustable spotlights on this cable system help keep it unobtrusive within the clean lines of the skylight. It also provides essential light for working at night at the central kitchen island.

■ CABLE FIXTURES

Cable systems work most successfully when they are not obvious. Semi-industrial and minimalist designs are good choices, as are those that allow for bulb rotation—allowing you to get the light where it is needed. Clip-on accessories can be used to focus light and prevent glare.

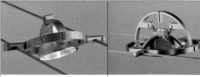

Standard halogen fully adjustable spotlight

Large fully adjustable super-spotlight

▶ Pools of light

A series of low-glare super spotlights provides focused pools of light over the kitchen's main workspace. The fixtures themselves can be moved along the cables to ensure the light falls where it is needed most. Despite a low ceiling, this cable solution blends well with this multi-layered interior.

▲ Design with light

Freeform spots suspended from a cable system can add visual interest to a space in their own right. Both are cowled to prevent glare.

CABLE OPTIONS

1 Simple downlights
Stretched between two points, a system that takes standard low-voltage 2-inch (50-mm) dichroic bulbs is useful for low ceilings.

2 Up/down combination
Use the larger bulbs for ceiling heights over 8½ feet (2.6 m). Reverse the fixtures to provide uplight options.

3 Vertical systems
Use a vertical system carefully to prevent glare. Fit accessories to direct the light where needed.

Adjustable tubular spotlight

Single mount for all planes

Double stand-off mount

Dedicated ceiling mount

Corner ceiling mount

Do
- Use cable systems to light artwork, provide general working light, and even uplight where no recess is available.
- Choose a system with clip-on lenses and louvers to prevent glare when fixtures cannot be ideally positioned (see page 67).
- Opt for silver-backed bulbs to prevent a pink back-glow.

Don't
- Use long stretches over 39 feet (12 m) without the additional supports that will be required.

▼ **Suspended magic**
A cable system with a difference creates visual impact in this double-height space. Powered from a wall plate, the fixtures hang without apparent support. This gives them an ethereal feel and provides useful light in a difficult-to-light space.

low-glare spot to light artwork. For uplighting choose a wide-beam bulb.

Most systems can be stretched over a distance of 33–36 feet (10–11 m). For longer distances you will need to provide additional support. The key is to ensure that you have two points to which the cables can be securely fixed. The cable is normally used horizontally—fixed to opposite walls of a room. However, in some situations it can also be used vertically.

As with a track system, some cable fixtures will allow you to use clip-on lenses and louvers. It is worth opting for this type, as this provides greater flexibility and ensures the end result is a more unobtrusive, low-glare light source.

You will need to consider the location of any transformer, which can be either wall mounted or—preferably—remote. The distance of the fixture from the transformer will need to be taken into account to prevent voltage drop.

Use cable systems to
- Provide discreet lighting for works of art and where no recess is available.
- Light even in the most difficult-to-light spaces.
- Direct light onto tables or kitchen islands from within skylights.

Cable systems in practice
Cable lighting works well when used in skylights to provide task lighting beneath—for example, over an island in a kitchen. Because a cable system is so minimal, it can be used in a traditional setting, such as a barn conversion, without detracting from the surroundings. Some systems have a variety of lamps to choose from.

▶ **Discreet pitch**
This classic cable system employs a high-wattage bulb to provide practical in-fill light in this pitched space without interfering with the simple regularity and clean lines of the beams.

Wall-mounted uplighting and downlighting

These options provide additional shadow-free light and can be an ideal solution where good working light is required.

Wall-mounted uplights and up/down lights (fixtures that will light both upward and downward) can be an economic way to get more light into a space or to provide sufficient practical light if you do not want to use recess lighting. The light sources that are most suitable for use in uplights or downlights are short, double-ended halogen tubes (see page 24) and the energy-saving compact fluorescent equivalents (see page 26). Halogen bulbs have the advantage of being easily dimmed. The light from a compact fluorescent bulb is cool in color. Seeking out a good-quality bulb will always provide a warm rather than cool, gray light. Dimmable versions of compact fluorescent bulbs are now available, making them more practical for use in bedrooms.

The best types of fixtures to choose are slim, architectural styles that will easily blend into a room. Often those in a raw-plaster finish are the most successful, having the advantage that you can paint the fixture to match the color of the wall. They are therefore suitable for both traditional and contemporary spaces. You will always need to leave a certain amount of space above the fixture to allow the light to reflect back into the room. A minimum of 12–20 inches (300–510 mm) is best, depending on the strength and type of bulb you choose to use.

LIGHT EMISSION

1. Straight up narrow
Use a narrow-beam uplight to highlight an architectural feature.

2. Wide wash up
A wide wash of uplight reflects off a ceiling to provide shadow-free light.

3. Straight up and down
Use several up/down lights to decorate a plain wall with a variety of beam widths.

4. Straight down
A straight downlight is useful for highlighting potted topiary or picking out structural details.

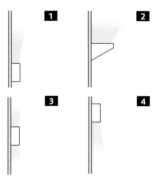

■ UPLIGHTS AND UP/DOWN LIGHTS

A minimalist look is easy to achieve with raw-plaster fixtures that allow you to paint them to blend easily with the decor or architecture of the room. Metal finishes provide the freedom to install these fixtures outdoors.

| Skinny tubular up- and downlight | Layered ceramic up- and downlight | Ring-shaped ceramic up- and downlight | Tall metal up- and downlight |

◀ Compact solution
A simple square up/down light provides a touch of drama to an otherwise utilitarian space.

▶ Clear space
Tubular up/down lights provide a dramatic background to the simplest of bathroom spaces. Narrow-beam bulbs create strong washes of light that frame the elevation, letting the light become the decoration. The crisp nickel finish of the fixtures blends well with the decor.

Up/down lights provide you with useful uplighting as well as an element of dramatic downlighting.

Plaster fixtures generally take a maximum incandescent bulb strength of 200 watts because of the heat this type of bulb generates. However, a 2 x 26-watt compact fluorescent fixture can be found in plaster designs and with simple colorful silk shades. The latter are very useful for disguising the cool tone of fluorescent bulbs.

Use wall-mounted uplights to
■ Boost shadow-free reflected light.
■ Provide a source of practical light where no recess is available.

◀ Neat fit
Contemporary fixtures can work in a traditional space. The up/down lights frame the window without imposing on the space or the surrounding architecture. The effect is to draw the eye both up and down, expanding the sense of space.

Little metal cube up- or downlight

Fabric shade up- and downlight

Wooden cube up- and downlight

Slim plaster uplight

Gently curved aluminum uplight

Bowl-shaped uplight

◄ **Regular rhythm**
The up/down lights complement the industrial tone of the space and bring out the color and texture of the brick wall. Use of multiple fixtures lends a serene softness to the hard textures of the space.

▼ **Practical minimalism**
Energy efficiency is made easy with the use of raw-plaster up/down lights that blend well into most spaces. Wired on their own circuit, the fixtures can be used to boost light levels when required, leaving other light sources to provide a softer, more moody feel in the evening.

Do
■ Leave plenty of space above the fixture for the light to dissipate.
■ Choose a good-quality compact fluorescent bulb for a warmer tone.
■ Use a downlight fixture with a diffuser to prevent the bulb from being seen.

Don't
■ Use wall-mounted uplights with low ceilings (height of less than 7¼ feet/2.2 m)

Spectacular simplicity
Both the up/down lights and low-level
floor washers used here are in keeping
with the architecture and provide all the
light required in this contemporary
extension to a historical building. Narrow-
beam bulbs add an extra "edge."

Practical tips

Wall-mounted up/down lights can improve the lighting in
many different ways in your home.

■ A pair of wall-mounted uplights can be used to frame
a bedroom wall (perhaps on either side of a closet) or can
be installed over a desk to provide sufficient practical light
to the room.

■ Supplemented with table lamps, the two layers of light
provided by an up/down light provide a convenient and
economic way to light a child's room or a guest bedroom.

Textured harmony
A raw-plaster rectangular light fixture to which a special wall finish has been applied blends into the wall, providing discreet and unobtrusive lighting that does not draw attention away from the sculpture.

Supporting role

Slim plaster fixtures provide ambient light and reinforce the focus given to the artwork by a ceiling-recessed spotlight. A square up/down light on the adjoining wall connects the dining area to the kitchen space beyond.

■ Double-height spaces are brought to life by the use of up/down lights, as they illuminate the architecture and help to keep open spaces connected.

■ A small cube-style downlight fixture is effective where space for a bedside reading light is limited, keeping the bedside table free of clutter. The best height at which to position this type of fixture depends on the type of bed you have and the height and width of the headboard. Around 43–50 inches (1.1–1.3 m) from the floor is a good height in most situations.

■ A square up/down light is a handy way to get light into the tight turn of a staircase without taking up much space. This type of fixture has the advantage of providing a glare-free light in a tricky space and is accessible for maintenance. You can either make a feature of this type of light by opting for a metal finish or use a plaster fixture that you can paint to match the wall.

Floor-recessed uplights and wall-recessed floor washers

Both floor-recessed uplights and wall-recessed floor washers are the tools of choice when a punchy insert of drama or a soft night-light is wanted.

Floor-recessed uplights are set into a floor void to skim light up an object or a vertical surface, such as a wall or the jamb of a fireplace. The light source must be positioned close to the wall or it will simply light space, as there will be nothing from which the light can reflect. Use this type of light to draw attention to architectural features such as archways, windows and fireplaces.

A wall-recessed floor washer is set flush into the wall at low level to provide a gentle general wash of light across the floor or across a stair tread. A good height for a wall-recessed floor washer from the finished floor level to the bottom of the fixture is about 9 inches (230 mm). This ensures the light is not so close to the step or floor that it creates a hot spot and not so high that its impact is lost. This form of lighting is ideal for lighting stairs and hallways and is an excellent source of light at night in a bathroom or child's bedroom.

These fixtures generally need a low-voltage source of light, which requires the addition of a transformer. Care must be taken to ensure that objects and fabrics do not come into contact with the fixture. Much-improved LED versions are now available to provide a cool-to-the-touch shaft of light, and these are an ideal choice for lighting areas where heat would be a problem. You will need to use

DIRECTION AND SPREAD OF LIGHT

1 Low-level wall-recessed floor wash
A wall-recessed floor washer will provide a gentle pool of light to bring out the color and texture of a floor.

2 Floor-recessed uplight
Floor-recessed uplights are positioned close to vertical elements, in this case the jambs, so the light skims the surface to draw the eye to a focal point.

3 Wall-recessed step washer
Set low, a wall-recessed step washer allows the light to hug a step or stair tread, creating a sense of added width, and draws the eye up the staircase to the space beyond.

■ LOW-LEVEL LIGHT FIXTURES

The evolution of the LED light source has enabled wall- and floor-recessed uplights to be miniaturized. Their much-reduced floor-recess depth makes them easier to install in most walls and floors for a useful additional layer of light. All these examples are LED.

Wall-recessed small floor washer

Wall-recessed standard-size floor washer

Wall-recessed slot floor washer

◄ **Night passage**
Low-level floor washers bring out the color and texture of the floor in this bathroom, providing a useful night-light or a gentle light when bathing.

these with a driver, and careful consideration should be given to recess depths.

Use floor-recessed uplighting to
■ Create fabulous focus for a fireplace or window reveal.
■ Backlight a sculpture or plinth.

Use wall-recessed floor washers to
■ Achieve stylish and practical low-level lighting on a staircase.
■ Provide a subtle source of light at night in bathrooms and along hallways.

▲ **Architectural accents**
Cool-to-the-touch uplights are set into a deep window frame to skim light up the shutters, softly picking out the details. The same type of fixture is used on the underside of the top of the frame to create a pool of light on the window ledge.

Floor- or wall-recessed uplight

Floor- or wall-recessed low-glare uplight

Floor- or wall-recessed eyelid uplight or floor washer

▶ **Stately progression**
Uplights framing the picture draw the eye along the length of this entrance. Pace is added into the space with the use of low-level floor washers, which provide a sense of progression.

▲ **Framed perfection**
The jambs of the fireplace are lit with uplights to provide a low-level highlight. The effect reinforces the fireplace as a focal point, providing visual balance to the painting above, which is lit from the ceiling with a low-voltage recessed spotlight.

Creating definition and focus

If a room is lacking in definition, a floor-recessed uplight will not only provide an additional layer of light but will also highlight objects of interest. Located in the joints, these lights will skim light up the divisions between bookshelves. They can also be used to uplight and pick out architectural details, such as those provided by archways and door frames. This can also be particularly effective in hallways, helping to draw the eye through the space.

To add interest to a sculpture or other work of art, position a floor-recessed uplight behind a plinth to throw the plinth and any object placed on it into silhouette. Alternatively, use this type of fixture on either side of an object of interest to frame it and give it prominence.

Step lights

Floor-recessed step lights provide light for steps where space does not allow wall lights and where it is not desirable to use recessed ceiling fixtures—for example, in

Do

■ Use cool sources of light near fabrics, shutters and windows.
■ Choose LED uplighters and floor washers where possible.
■ Pick out focal points such as fireplaces using uplighting.

Don't

■ Use hot sources of light where people might walk barefoot.
■ Fit floor-recessed or wall-recessed floor washers in showers. No subsequent seal between the fixture and tiling will be tight enough for safety.

Low-level connection
Recessed into the kick plate of a kitchen island, low-level fixtures provide a gentle wash of light that highlights the color and texture of the floor. This is also a useful source of light to connect the dining and cooking areas. The low-level light layer is complemented by wall-mounted up/down lights and low-glare ceiling-recessed spotlights. The result is a textured and layered lighting solution in this practical kitchen space.

◄ Plug-in highlights

LED uplights are recessed into the joints to highlight the cornice detail. This is a great way to insert definition and highlights into a space if you cannot start from scratch; the fixtures can always be run from a socket point.

▲ Stair definition

Square wall-recessed step washers provide practical and stylish light that works in harmony with the strict architectural lines of the staircase.

sloping ceilings. A low-voltage version will provide a gentle, dimmable wash of light over the step. This source has the added advantage of picking out the color and texture of the floor material.

If you decide to opt for the energy-efficient LED version of the floor light, be sure to pick out a warm white color, as opposed to a cool-colored version. This will ensure that the floor or step material will appear true to its original color when lit. The LED version is also the best choice when a night-light is required, as it can be left on for long periods of time without getting hot or consuming large amounts of electricity.

When set into a staircase, a cylindrical floor or step light will skim light across the step, indicating a change in floor height and adding to the layers of light in the space. It is best to light wide steps with a narrow, focused beam.

▼ **Balancing act**

This low-level floor washer provides an ideal night-light in this bathroom and is complemented by a linear light source concealed under the bench seat. The resulting effect balances the cool, chunky stonework. Ceiling-recessed low-glare spotlights highlight the mirror and framed artwork (seen in the reflection).

▶ **Small but beautiful**

Iridescent tiles spring to life as the low-level floor washers reflect light off the walls. Flush under-cabinet lights highlight the niche behind the toilet, providing a second level of visual interest.

Concealed lighting

Concealed lighting can add practical as well as soothing light to a space. It is also a way of creating a dramatic, mysterious or magical atmosphere.

A concealed light can provide a soothing, soft light or a more practical, hard-working effect, depending on what light source is chosen for the task. This form of lighting naturally lends itself for use within existing items in a room, such as in or on top of bookshelves or armoires, and makes ideal additional lighting for an existing scheme. For instance, you can use a concealed light source on top of kitchen cabinets to provide much of the practical light you need in a kitchen. Be sure to allow at least 12 inches (30 cm) of space between the light source and the ceiling so the light can reflect effectively. If you plan to use a lot of built-in shelving, it is worth considering the addition of concealed lighting at the time of designing the units. The light will then "lift" the units, preventing them from looking too heavy.

You can also apply techniques for concealed lighting to low-voltage downlights by placing them behind a dropped ceiling section (see also Cove and Coffer Lighting, pages 108–113). An example of this application is in a shower where the fixtures skim light downward without any apparent light source being visible.

Concealed light also works well in historic buildings that were not designed with electric light in mind. This is because light can be added to the existing structures or features without having to disturb the fabric of the room.

Soft seclusion
A gentle glow at the bedside is created using rope lights set vertically either side of the shelves. Side-stands conceal the source, leaving a non-distracting bedside light to highlight the feature and to provide the useful addition of a reading light.

■ FIXTURES FOR CONCEALED LIGHTING

LED sources are the first choice for concealed lighting. Improved color rendition and very long life (up to 50,000 hours) make LEDs a practical as well as aesthetic solution. Their miniature size requires only very small features to hide them. Low-voltage and standard-voltage light sources can also provide useful solutions.

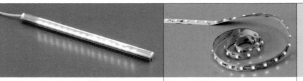

LED linear strip with optic diffuser

Flexible LED linear contour strip

Defined silhouette
A soft backlight is achieved with the use of concealed low-voltage click strip lighting to throw up a warm light behind a series of blue and white china jars. The low-voltage light source brings out the color of the jars and provides both a bright, practical light and a softer light, when dimmed, for an atmospheric touch.

Choice of light source

Linear light sources are the best types of light to use in restricted spaces. These can be fluorescent, low voltage, standard voltage or LED. A low-voltage or fluorescent light source is best used where strong light is required—for example, on top of kitchen cabinets or bookshelves. A standard-voltage soft light provides an excellent night-light when wrapped around the underside of a bed and offset from the floor by at least 6 inches (15 cm).

Use concealed light to

■ Create subtle lighting effects.
■ Provide practical boosts of light.
■ Produce a low-level night-light.
■ Soften existing lighting and provide an additional layer of light for long runs of built-in bookshelves.

Lighting through glass

You can have a lot of fun employing concealed light sources to create dramatic effects. For example, consider using a linear LED source behind chunky white glass shelves to create contemporary bookcase lighting. For best effect, remember to frost the front of the shelves to stop the light from traveling all the way through the glass. This also works well in a bathroom where a

CONCEALING LIGHTS IN SHELVING

Adding a down-stand
When installing light into a shelving unit, it is important to ensure the fixture cannot be seen. A down-stand of 1½ inches (4 cm) will ensure that either low-voltage or standard voltage fixtures are concealed.

Adding an up-stand
If uplighting, add an up-stand, unless the fixture is set so high that it cannot be seen from any angle in the room. LED light sources may not need an up-stand.

Routed-out groove
A discreet way to incorporate any source of linear light into shelving is to create a groove in the shelf. This ensures the front edge remains seamless for a better overall finish. Always check that the light source cannot be seen from below.

| Fluorescent T5 bulb | Flexible mains voltage rope light | Low-voltage fixed strip |

cantilevered glass shelf can appear to float by using the same lighting solution.

Softening edges

Bookshelves can be lit with concealed linear or horizontal light sources to add an intermediate layer of light to a space and soften the presence of joints. You can apply the same principles as lighting at low level to lighting around a kitchen island or under cantilevered benches. This is a great way to introduce light to produce a soft wash of light over the floor, softening hard surfaces. The light will also double up as a night-light.

Another option is to position lights on top of a bookshelf, armoire or kitchen cabinets for an easy-to-achieve shadow-free reflected light that, when dimmed, adds a warm glow to the room in the evening.

In both these options, it is important to remember that the effect will be ruined if the light source is not properly concealed. In some cases you may need to incorporate a side-stand (if running light vertically in bookshelves) or a down-stand (if using the light source horizontally under

▲ Edge lit
Floating glass shelves add an eye-catching yet minimalistic touch to a bathroom. Frosting the front and side edges stops the colored light from traveling farther, creating a line of colored light.

◄ Soft drop
The concealed light set within this dropped ceiling coffer lends a sophisticated feel to this bedroom. The dropped section conceals a standard-voltage linear light source that gives the room a soft wash of downlight. Using a dropped coffer in this way provides the opportunity to lower very high ceilings and to add light in historic buildings where it is not possible to recess light fixtures.

Concealed opportunities

Linear light sources can be run horizontally under the front edge of shelves for a soft wash of light (far left). This works best to light books. Used behind chunky glass or Plexiglas shelves, they will create a more contemporary, floating effect, even in a traditional setting (near left). A more three-dimensional look is achieved by setting shelves forward and concealing the light source directly behind each shelf. This adds instant depth to the space and draws the eye (below left).

Do

■ Consider using this type of light source in historic buildings to create a natural effect.
■ Use this type of lighting when you want minimal clutter or where space is limited.

Don't

■ Use concealed lighting close to a shiny floor surface. You will see the light source reflected in the floor, ruining the effect.
■ Install low-level linear concealed lighting in an area where it may end up simply lighting an unsightly floor, such as in a kitchen.

individual shelves, bench seats or at low level under a kitchen island, see page 103). Where concealed light is used under individual shelves, it is a good idea to allow a down-stand of at least 1¼–1½ inches (32–39 mm) to make sure the fixtures cannot be seen while you are seated.

Glamour and magic

Use a standard-voltage rope light under beds for instant nighttime glamour or under the nosing of step treads. Do take any reflections you might get into account and remember to consider that any piece of furniture may well need to be moved from time to time, so it is worth fitting a floor socket so you can use a plug-in fixture.

Concealed light around the edge of a coffee table can be used to create the impression that it is "floating." This can add a stunning focal point to a room and is particularly useful in double-height spaces, where it may be difficult to provide light to a central seating area. Again, you will need to consider fitting a floor socket.

▲ Floating options
A modern treatment of the hole-in-the-wall fireless fireplace uses concealed linear lights to draw the eye and highlight the objects within. The bench in front of the fireplace is brought alive by concealing an LED linear light source beneath it (above left). The same effect is achieved using a simple standard-voltage rope light under a coffee table to create a stunning focal point (above). Because this is a plug-in solution, the table can easily be moved.

► Clean sweep
The overlapping and concealed dimmable fluorescent tubes under the long vanity prevent it from becoming an overly dominant feature in the space. The fixtures are set far enough off the floor to keep reflections from spoiling the effect.

Cove and coffer lighting

The introduction of a soft, linear light into a recessed area, such as a cove or ceiling coffer, is an ideal way to add subtle background light to a room.

There are several types of light sources that can be used in a cove or ceiling coffer to add ambient light and increase the amount of general light in a room, to provide a diffused background light or to highlight an interesting architectural detail.

A linear fluorescent strip is a reasonably priced light source that will boost practical light in, for example, a kitchen. Click strip is a low-voltage linear light source that uses miniature xenon bulbs and gives a crisp white light when used at full strength. It can also be dimmed to produce a more mellow color, which works well in living areas. A standard-voltage rope light provides a warm yellow light but does not give a huge output, and it is best used in shelves and along the joints in furniture. The most energy-efficient linear light source suited to this task is LED. The best type of LED to use in this situation is one that gives off a warm rather than cool light. This type of light has the added advantage of a long life span—up to 50,000 hours.

Positioning the light source

Most of the ideal light sources for coves and coffers are small and compact and lend themselves to being used even in the smallest

Soft definition
A standard-voltage linear rope light is concealed in this bathroom coffer to give a wash of soft light over the slightly domed ceiling. This wash of gentle light is a perfect background light for the evening and highlights the unusual architectural detail.

COFFERS AND DROPPED CEILINGS

Standard coffer
The ideal dimensions for your coffer will depend on what source of light you want to use. Leave plenty of room between the light source and the ceiling to allow the light to diffuse, and consider where to locate drivers or transformers before you begin.

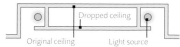

Dropped ceiling
The same rules apply as for fitting a light in a standard coffer. However, the depth of the drop and the distance from the edge of the ceiling are important in order to ensure the room still feels balanced. You will need to ensure you can access the fixtures so you can change bulbs when necessary.

■ FIXTURES

See Concealed Lighting, pages 103–104.

of spaces. Light can be positioned on top of wall paneling for a soft uplight. In this case, a small up-stand may be required to hide the light source. A discreet way to uplight in confined, narrow spaces, such as hallway entrances, is to use a specially designed cornice with light set within it. Where a ceiling can be dropped, a small coffer design allows light to be run around the sides of the room, providing a soft addition of light. You will need at least 12 inches (30 cm) between the light source and the ceiling to ensure the light has enough space to dissipate and to maximize the reflected light. The smaller the distance between the light source and the ceiling, the harder the light source will appear. In other words, it will become more like a line of light around the room instead of providing the intended gentle glow. Paint

Vaulted connection
A low-voltage light source has been run along either side of this barrel-vaulted ceiling to create the illusion of extra height and to act as a link between the seating and dining areas. When the light is at full strength, it provides a practical level of light to the space, and when dimmed it creates a beautifully relaxed background light.

the inner part of the coffer matte white to ensure maximum reflection of light back into the room. Also, the design of the coffer or cove is important. You need to be sure that the fixture itself will not be visible, even as a reflection in glass.

Lighting dropped ceilings
You can also drop the central part of a ceiling and use a linear light source to provide a diffused light. The gap should be at least

12 inches (30 cm) around the edges. This treatment works well in a large room with a ceiling height of over 8 feet (2.4 m) or along a narrow hallway. It is not suitable for ceilings lower than this because it can make the ceiling feel lower than it actually is, creating a rather oppressive feeling.

Use cove and coffer lighting as
■ A subtle addition of background light.
■ A main source of light when you wish to keep visual clutter to a minimum.

Choosing the light source
The type of light source you choose will depend on what type of effect you want to create. The following are the main options:
■ Linear fluorescent is an economic choice that adds to the general lighting level, which is useful in a home office or a playroom. It is worth slightly overlapping the long bulbs to prevent blank spots and using a dimmer mechanism, known as a ballast (which can be hidden in the coffer), to give yourself more flexibility throughout the day. A warm white color of light is suitable for a playroom, while

Get advice
The success of this type of lighting is all in the details, and it is worth consulting a lighting designer if you are unsure about how to use it to best effect.

◄ **Supporting role**
This coffered ceiling is lit with a linear low-voltage light source, which adds softness to an otherwise strictly structured space. The light source is on its own circuit and can be dimmed. Low-voltage spotlights, recessed into the center of the ceiling, focus light onto the center of the table.

▶ **Great expectations**
A dropped ceiling, which conceals a linear LED light source, provides dramatic reflected light and adds a sense of grandeur to this hallway. Despite the narrowness of the space, this treatment is effective because of the height of the ceiling. The low-level floor washers serve to balance the light within the space.

Do

■ Paint the inner sections of coffers, coves and dropped ceiling sections matte white to maximize the light output.

■ Experiment with the dimensions of the coffer to ensure you do not see the light source or its reflection.

■ Take maintenance into account.

■ Overlap light sources to prevent gaps and blank spots.

Don't

■ Use coffers, coves or dropped ceilings where your existing ceiling is below 8 feet (2.4 m).

a cool daylight white works better in a laundry room.

■ Cold cathode, which has a long life span, provides a solution in hard-to-reach areas, such as a coffered ceiling over a staircase where access for maintenance may be difficult. Not generally used in homes, it is still worth considering for larger installations. Individual cold cathode fixtures are made to measure and can be created in curves for circular applications. A wide range of colors are available, from warm to cool.

■ A standard-voltage linear light source such as rope light, provides a pleasing soft yellow light and is ideal for use on top of paneling and around furniture joints. Often made to measure, it gives a similar light to that of a table lamp and provides an atmospheric glow in the evening. This type of light source can also be flexible enough to be bent into a circle or other shape, if required.

■ Low-voltage linear light sources in thin

metal strips on which small xenon bulbs are fitted are a versatile option because they provide bright light during the day and a mellow light when dimmed in the evening. This is useful when a space has to serve more than one function—for example, a playroom by day that doubles up as a media room during the evening.

■ A warm-colored linear LED is hard to beat for a truly energy-efficient and low-maintenance solution. Its tiny size—often less than ½ inch (13 mm) wide and ¼ inch (6 mm) high—makes it easy to use in even the smallest of spaces. If you want to light a curved coffer, you will need to opt for an "edge lit" type. These also have a very long life, and there is a dimmable version that is suitable for most applications.

▲ Counterbalance
A concealed standard-voltage light source sits on top of paneling and provides a gentle light for bathing. It highlights the architectural detail, offering a softening counterpoint to the weighty marble tub in the center of the room.

◄ Light touch
This bathroom demonstrates how concealed lighting can easily be layered with other sources of light to create depth and texture. A standard-voltage rope light is concealed within the ceiling cove, while pairs of bold wall lights frame the mirrors. Individual low-voltage recessed lights highlight the mirrors.

► Pitched perfection
Effective but simply concealed low-voltage xenon fixtures sit on top of a run of wardrobes behind the main bedroom, uplighting the cathedral-like proportions of the space. The light has ample room to diffuse and displays the impressive proportions of the space, but when dimmed it creates a warm, cozy feel despite the height of the pitched ceiling.

Slot and niche lighting

This option is a clever way to inject pools of dramatic light into small spaces, slot and niche lighting. It can also be used to introduce focal points at eye level.

Well-lit slots, niches and alcoves, whether existing architectural features or purpose-made, offer an opportunity to add an extra dimension to a space. Cut into a wall, niches can be any shape or size and can run either horizontally or vertically. The light source can either sit in the top of or at the bottom of the slot or niche, and each position creates a very different effect. You can also light these areas from above and below, but you may want to put the sources on different circuits to allow more flexibility to control the final effect.

Uses and effects

Slots and niches can be designed to simply house light sources, or they can be made larger to create a platform to display objects. Remember that if you want to display an object and uplight from the bottom of the slot, you will need to ensure that there is enough room to position the object in front of the light source so as not to mask it. If you want to uplight through a glass object, such as a vase, you need to use a cool source of light, such as an LED. It is best to avoid lighting a vase or bowl from above; the light is likely to be "lost" inside the object. This is not a problem when lighting solid objects, which will reflect the light.

■ FITTINGS

See Fixed recessed downlights, pages 64–69

▲ **Classic highlight**
A classically shaped vase is highlighted with directional spotlights, positioned so as to cross-light the object. The fixtures are set in front of the object, so the light source bathes the front of the object with light.

▲ **Practical glamour**
The mirror-backed niches in this bathroom, created to house the radiators, receive an injection of glamour with the simple addition of an overhead low-voltage downlight.

▶ Added depth

A series of top-lit niches in this bathroom add depth to the space, drawing the eye toward the objects displayed within. They provide the main source of light in the room, allowing less lighting to be used in the ceiling. When dimmed, they are an indirect source of soft light. The niches in the shower provide useful shelf space.

SLOT LIGHTING IN PRACTICE

Decide if you need a linear or a direct spotlight source. If using a linear solution, ensure the fixtures can be hidden and the bulbs are not reflected into the surrounding surfaces. If you choose low-voltage spots, select the right voltage and beam width.

1 Vertical slot.
2 Uplit slot or niche.
3 Cross-down lit slot or niche.
4 Horizontal slot lit with miniature spotlights.
5 Horizontal slot lit with a linear light source.

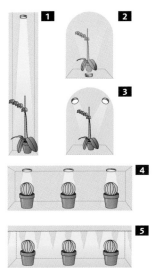

Use slot lighting to

■ Effectively display tools or objects.
■ Introduce a different layer of light.
■ Provide depth, texture and drama in an otherwise uneventful space.
■ Light an area of limited space.

In bathrooms

Large slots and niches can contain glass shelves on which to display objects. Lit from above with a low-voltage light, these can make a great feature in a bathroom, behind the toilet or on either side of the vanity. Use good-quality white glass (with a low iron content) to avoid a green glow. In bathrooms, niches provide useful shelves and minimize the need for overhead light. A long, horizontal slot in the wall behind a bath can provide a useful shelf as well as a relaxing light to bathe by.

In staircases

Another great application for slot lighting is in staircases, where they are a great way to introduce light without impinging on the sense of space. In narrow staircases,

◀ ▲ Slot power
This bedroom (seen without niches at left) is transformed by the introduction of top-lit display niches either side of the bed (above) These provide both an eye-catching sense of depth and a strong framing element for the bed itself.

▶ Welcoming warmth
A cozy and welcoming combination of layered light provides a focus to the headboard. A display alcove behind the bed is lit with LED recessed under-cabinet lights, while LED top-lit slots on either side of the bed provide an understated and cool-to-the-touch reading light.

linear slots running parallel to the stairs turn a functional space into a dramatic focal point and draw the eye upward, providing a sense of space.

In bedrooms

In bedrooms, slots and niches can double up as bedside tables or, above a headboard, can provide a shelf for books and the light source can be used as a bedside reading light. This keeps surfaces clean and minimal. In hallways, an occasional niche that contains soft light is a useful focal point and can lift an otherwise bland and uninteresting space. In areas where a restful source of light is required or where it is better to omit an overhead light, such as in a steam room, a niche that contains an interesting object can be lit to create a visual focal point.

Two-way draw

The lit slot concept is just as successful in outside spaces. Here, top-lit niches introduce useful low-glare light into a compact deck area. They also serve to pull the eye toward the view. LED uplights recessed into the deck beyond provide a visual counterbalance.

Outdoor slots

You can also create impact by introducing niches, slots and lit recesses outdoors. This is easier to do if you are constructing hard landscape elements from scratch (such as the wall pictured below). Such an approach enhances space and provides background light to a dining area, for example, without impinging on precious floor space. Use an easy-maintainance, low-voltage or LED fixture that is suitable for outside installation to achieve the effect.

Do

■ Use a low-glare source of light. If you can see into the niche, you don't want to be able to see the light source.
■ Consider whether it is most suitable to place the light in the top or the bottom of the slot or niche —or both.

Don't

■ Use hot sources of light in the bottom of a niche if you are placing objects on top.

Mirror lighting

Great lighting for a mirror is achieved by using a combination of light sources positioned correctly to provide both definition and flatter skin tones.

How to light bathroom mirrors to best effect is one of the most frequently asked questions when people are looking to improve their lighting. To achieve basic good light to a bathroom mirror, you need to combine low-voltage light from above with standard-voltage lights on either side. The position of the light above is critical in order to avoid unsightly shadows. You need the light to hit the mirror and reflect back to your face. You can achieve this by positioning a low-voltage directional spot in line with the edge of the vanity or sink. This will ensure the light can hit the mirror and bounce back to you. Always have the overhead lighting and the side lighting on separate circuits to allow you to control how much of each type you want at any one time.

Wide mirrors

If the mirror is wide or in your prime place for applying makeup or shaving, it is worth considering installing two directional low-voltage spotlights, ideally set approximately 24–31 inches (60–80 cm) apart and angled so the beams meet in the center of the mirror

If you have a really wide mirror, or individual mirrors hung over a pair of sinks, consider using three wall lights —one on each side and one in the middle to ensure an even spread of light.

▲ Side effect
Suitably sealed wall lights are used to give a soft light to both sides of the face while at the mirror. Mounted on the mirror, the chrome backplates blend seamlessly with the taps and faucets. Overhead ceiling-recessed directional spotlights are separately circuited for light to the sinks.

IDEAL MIRROR LIGHTING

The light from two medium-beam bulbs above the mirror crosses and is reflected back to the face. Lighting from both sides of the mirror provides infill and removes shadows.

■ LIGHT FIXTURES FOR MIRROR LIGHTS

Bathroom wall lights come in all shapes and sizes. Choose fixtures that complement your scheme. Be aware of the type of bulb the fixture is designed to hold. A fluorescent source will certainly give a bright light, but this can be harsh. An incandescent source is softer and more flattering and better for enhancing skin tone.

Frosted tungsten flush-to-wall

Frosted fluorescent flush-to-wall

Frosted mains voltage, stands proud

Frosted mains voltage hanging lamp

▶ **Clean sweep**

A mirror set slightly proud allows for semi-recessed mini spotlights to be set vertically either side of it. The result is a diffused but bright light, which when used at full-strength provides an excellent makeup light and, when dimmed, provides a soft, flattering light. Low-level floor washers are a good night-light and add balance.

▲ **Balanced light**

A pair of bathroom wall lights, set either side of this tall vertical mirror, add a structured "masculine" feel to the space. Ideally positioned, the incandescent light source enhances skin tone and provides a good light for shaving. An overhead recessed directional spotlight lifts the light level and highlights the sink.

Mirror with integral fluorescent lights

Overarching main voltage mirror light

Octagonal wall light

Shaded fluorescent adjustable light

Swing arm bathroom wall light

Capsule light with reflective backplate

Avoiding shadows

Overhead lighting will always give you fairly accurate light to the face but with shadows under the nose and the chin. To eradicate these shadows, add a pair of standard-voltage wall lights to introduce a soft layer of intermediate light, which also improves skin tones.

If you have no recess in the ceiling for an overhead light, consider partially recessing a 20-watt/12-volt mini spotlight with a reflective backplate into the mirror. This type of fixture can provide a high level of diffused light overall and, when dimmed, a softer, more flattering light. Position the fixture either above eye level (approximately 6½ feet/2 m from the floor level) or down either side of the mirror.

▶ **Face lift**
There are many sources of light that you can use around the focal point of a mirror to provide depth and texture to a space. It is a particularly softening tool in a room with many surfaces that are smooth, flat and hard.

1 Overhead light
A ceiling-recessed directional spotlight set in line with the edge of the vanity provides the best practical light.

2 Side light
Stylish ceiling-hung lights provide a different take on bathroom wall lights and give soft side lighting to the face.

3 Side light and low-level light
A further layer of light washes the vanity and draws attention to crystal objects on its surface. The low-level light is balanced by the hanging lights.

4 Overhead light and side light
A combination of ceiling-recessed and side lights provide ideal face lighting. The side lights can be dimmed and the overhead spot turned off for a more relaxed atmosphere.

◀ **Low-key solution**
Concealing a light source behind the mirror creates a low-key feel in the decorative scheme and produces a wonderfully restful glow. If you use this solution with a very large mirror, it is important to add correctly positioned overhead lighting to provide practical light to the face.

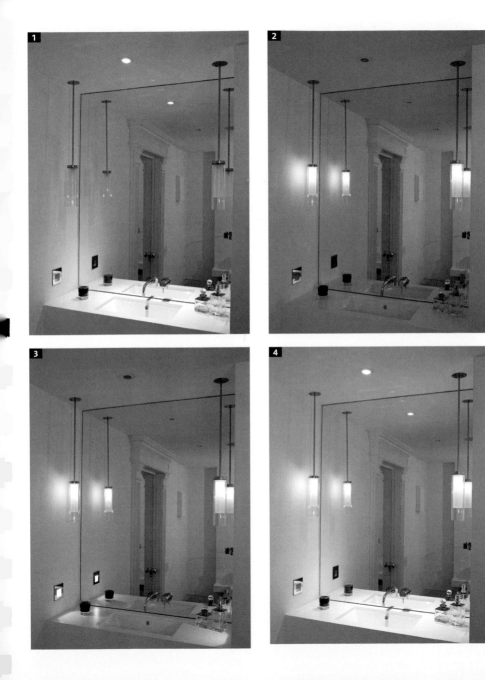

Other options

A more understated option is to use a linear light source set in a recess and mount the mirror surface overtop, flush with the edge of the recess. This will give a diffused side light around the edge of the mirror and be a useful night-light. A low-voltage linear light source is suited to this purpose. For energy efficiency, opt for a linear LED.

If you have the luxury of a custom-made built-in dressing table, it is best to connect your light sources to a locally positioned dimmer switch, which will allow you to conveniently alter the light levels to suit the task at hand. If you use a stand-alone dressing table with a mirror set on top, it is a good idea to place a table lamp on each side of the mirror to provide a balanced light.

A mirror hung over a fireplace will reflect back any natural light entering the room during the day, but at night it can lack sparkle. A single low-voltage directional spot will bring it back to life. Even an antique mirror will benefit from this treatment.

Use mirror lighting to
- Provide the best light to the face.
- Add a separate layer of light within a space.
- Draw attention to a focal point.

Do
- Consider the locations of all the light sources in the room.
- Combine different levels of light sources to provide the best lighting to your face.
- Use adequate amounts of light. A dimmer can be fitted to reduce light levels when less light is required.

Don't
- Position light sources in the ceiling in front or behind where you will stand to look into a mirror. This will give more shadow than light.

Simple reflection
A single ceiling-recessed spotlight adds a subtle sparkle to this mirror. It also serves to reflect other light sources in the room, ensuring the mirrored surface does not appear flat and dull.

Practical tips

When lighting the mirrors in your home, bear the following considerations in mind:

■ As long as it is well positioned, the more light you have, the better the light to your face will be. A single directional spot provides the essential light. You can always experiment with wall lights, as these will make a strong style statement and provide essential side lighting to the face.

■ A backlit mirror is often most successful with a mosaic-tiled surround, as this will also add sparkle.

■ Lights hung from the ceiling can provide an alternative to wall-mounted lights to give side lighting to the face.

Sitting pretty

A welcoming glow radiates from this expertly lit living room. A ceiling-recessed spotlight subtly picks out the mirror as a focal point without detracting from the essential warmth of the table lamps, the gentle sparkle from the chandelier and the beautifully highlighted paintings.

■ The best type of light to choose is often a frosted glass tubular design, which will allow the light to dissipate sideways, where you need it most.

■ A full-length back-lit mirror in a dressing room can provide a simple, understated facility to check an outfit as well as provide a focal point for the room.

Task lighting

Well-designed task lighting is an important foundation for a well-functioning room. The key to successful task lighting is choosing the right source of light for the job and positioning the source exactly where it is required.

Many types of light sources can be employed for task lighting depending on where the source is required and exactly what it is needed for. Low-voltage bulbs always provide a crisp light, but LED lighting now provides highly effective solutions for task light because of its small size and low heat output. However, it is hard to beat a traditional standard-voltage desk light for providing functionality and atmosphere as well as something stylish to look at.

Lighting a working space

You can use under-cabinet lights—either LED or low-voltage—to light work surfaces or compact desk units. These can be surface mounted or, for a cleaner finish, semi-recessed into the base of a wall-mounted unit or shelf. It is important to ensure against glare by using a shielded light source. A linear light source is also suitable for task lighting in these situations, although you need to be careful to avoid reflections in computer screens or from reflective work surfaces. Opt for wall-mounted flexible lights over a desk

Adjustable style
A stylish classic desk light is easy to adjust to suit whatever the working conditions dictate. A honeycomb louver (right) softens the light and reduces reflections from paper and computer screens for an ideal working light.

■ TASK LIGHT FIXTURES

Consider the location where you need your task light—over a desk, in a sitting room or at a bedside—and this will help you decide what type of fixture will suit your needs the best.

Desklamp

Wall-mounted LED adjustable spot

Floor-standing adjustable light

◀ Slim fit
Flush under-cabinet lights, recessed into wall-mounted kitchen units, provide uninterrupted working light directly to the counters in this kitchen. If on a separate circuit, they can be dimmed for a convenient light source for early-morning and late-evening kitchen activity as well as provide good task light at any time.

▼ Discreet sparkle
Practical light from under-cabinet lights recessed into the base of this bathroom unit adds sparkle to the colored-glass vanity top and the surrounding tiles. It also prevents the overhanging cabinet from casting a dark shadow over the sinks.

positioned next to a wall or a cabinet to save space on the desk surface.

Bedroom and bathroom

In the bedroom, a highly focused light, such as a flexible pin-spot LED, enables you to read without disturbing the person next to you. You can add a bedside table lamp to provide a low-level layer of atmospheric light.

Always consider putting some form of lighting in your closets, particularly if these are of dark wood. Use a cool light source, such as linear daylight-white fluorescent bulbs. These will help you distinguish between dark colors. Shield the light source to reduce

Traditional adjustable-arm wall light

Fixed shielded under-cabinet light

any glare and use a door-operated switch for convenience.

In the bathroom, a well-positioned backlit wall-mounted magnifying mirror is a useful tool to add, particularly for shaving, although it is no substitute for lighting a mirror well (see pages 118–123).

Use task lighting to

■ Provide specific and sufficient light to read or work by.

■ Create localized pools of light that can be used without having to alter the light levels in the rest of a room.

▲ **Flexible focus**
A flexible pin-spot LED can be mounted to the wall or fixed to the headboard (inset) to provide a well-positioned source of light for reading. The narrow beam focuses light on the page without disturbing the person on the other side of the bed.

◀ **Compact solution**
In the bedroom, a bedside reading light is wall mounted to maximize space on the bedside table. The jointed arm allows the light to be pulled out for better positioning of the light when reading and folded back for a neat finish during the day.

Do

■ Consider the location of the task light. If positioned even slightly too high or too low it will fail to fulfill its function.
■ Install a local control for the light source.

Don't

■ Attempt to provide task lighting by increasing lighting levels in the room as a whole.

▲ Design classic
Nothing beats this perfect combination of form and function. An Anglepoise light not only looks good, it provides the flexibility required for practical reading light.

Task lighting tips

■ An LED wall-mounted bedside reading light pools a concentrated source of light onto a page of a book. The advantage of using LEDs in this situation is that a cool-to-the-touch light source is always a better option near bare arms or fabrics.

■ A light source for task lighting can be suspended from the ceiling to give a decorative finish. Just remember that you want to use the light source to read by, not just to light the bedside table.

■ Use a series of shielded recessed under-cabinet lights in the first shelf over a desk. This puts the light where you need it without using up valuable desk space. This solution also works well under wall-mounted kitchen cabinets to provide good light to the countertops.

■ A freestanding plug-in light can provide reading light in a living room without disrupting atmospheric lighting. This is also the perfect solution if you want to add a localized boost of light to a games table, for example.

▲ Floor-standing flexibility
An individual task light is easily incorporated into the seating area of a living room for reading (top) or board games (above) by the addition of a fully adjustable floor light. An internal reflector in the head of the fixture boosts the light output, and the shape reduces glare.

Special effects lighting

A selection of carefully planned lighting techniques, or "tricks," including color changes and night-sky effects, will add that extra special wow factor to any lighting scheme.

Experiment with color as a fun tool to add drama to a room or to create a specific atmosphere. Color has a powerful effect on mood. For example, add blue and green tones to create a cool feeling, warm tones in the red/pink spectrum for relaxation and use yellow/orange tones to provide a cheerful, "sunny" atmosphere.

Matching the fixture to the location
Linear LED white light or a color-changing version known as RGB (red, green, blue) can be fitted behind a frosted glass or Plexiglas backsplash in a kitchen or panel on the side of a bathtub. The small size of LED systems and their long life makes them a practical choice for such an installation. The RGB source can be operated by remote control to scroll through the colors, or it can be stopped on a particular color for a dramatic static effect. It is always worth fitting the option of a white source for when a calmer, practical light is required.

The best low-cost light sources are gel-wrapped standard-voltage linear fluorescent bulbs, which can easily be used as a

Color in view
Fitting colored lights behind a screen is an excellent way to make the space "active" when the TV is not in use. You can install a variety of color options to suit your mood.

▲ **Primary objective**
Bold primary colors create instant party spaces. You don't need to mix lots of different colors—a single color can be very effective—but for a really special effect, a multiple-color facility is a great tool.

▶ **Subtle hues**
A calm and stylish effect is achieved through the use of pale purple hues. Choose hues of a different color if you want to change the mood.

▲ Outer space
Fiber optics have been used to create a stunning starry-sky effect over this indoor swimming pool.

▶ Nightscape
The ultimate night-light for a child's bedroom, this gentle effect is achieved by using a scattering of fiber optics in the ceiling.

replacement light source or as a plug-in addition in an existing lighting scheme.

If you are starting from scratch, consider using either low-voltage or metal-halide fiber optics. These can be used set into a floor to create your own dance floor or in a ceiling to reproduce a starry-sky effect.

Budget-friendly options

Naturally, some of the best effects cost a lot, but you can still inject unusual drama into a space on a budget. This can be achieved by using a plug-in fluorescent tube covered with a slip-on gel sleeve. As fluorescents are a cool source of light, it is safe to leave them behind

▲ Meteoric effect
A private universe has been created in this combined living room, media room and den. The "out of this world" effect uses an uplit ceiling coffer and colored linear lights in the organic-shaped display niches.

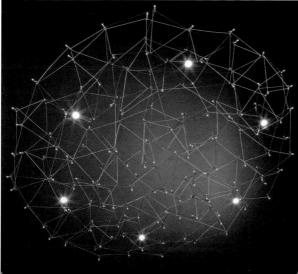

◄ Bespoke universe
A decorative fixture, such as this "universe" effect, can be designed with LED or fiber optics to create a unique and dramatic addition to a space.

Shadow play
Fiber optics twinkle within the planter to create a play of shadow and light on a clean, feature-free wall, offering a counterpoint to the hard lines of the glass and stone stairway.

sheer curtains or a piece of furniture for an easy and temporary dynamic effect. You can also change the gel sleeve when you are in the mood for a different color. The same method can be used to create mood-changing light behind your headboard (see pages 60–61).

Tips for using special effects

■ Create a starry-sky effect with fiber optics. This is an excellent effect for ceilings over indoor swimming pools, in steam rooms, over hot tubs and over children's beds as a night-light.

■ Enhance a starry sky by using a "twinkle wheel" to create a sparkling light effect.

■ Vary the size of the stars. A larger fiber end can be used to represent the larger planets, while smaller fiber ends can represent the stars. Using a mix of the two will create a more realistic effect.

■ Go for accurate astronomy. You could replicate an actual star constellation, perhaps reflecting astrological star signs, as an original way to personalize a space.

■ Use fiber optics to inject color onto large expanses of white walls. Use a color wheel to introduce several colors and cycle them.

■ Don't limit yourself to bold primary colors; you can use a wide range of subtle hues and tones to create a more thoughtful effect.

■ In outside spaces, strap optical fibers around ground-recessed water jets to create your own light and water show. As the jets are activated, the light will dramatically illuminate the water source.

■ Inset colored fiber optics into window reveals or niches for seasonal celebrations— for example, use reds and greens around Christmas time or sunny yellow for a summer evening party.

Colored contours

Outside spaces often provide a great opportunity to add a splash of colored light. This outdoor feature lit in vivid shades of rose provides a contemporary counterpoint to the flower beds beyond.

Do

■ Use the services of a lighting designer to help you make the most of a special effect. It is worth the investment to get exactly what you want.

■ Experiment with color.

■ Remember that you will have to live with any permanently fitted special effects. Pink uplights may look good for a party, but they are less useful for everyday lighting.

Don't

■ Overdo it. The effect will only be special if used where you really want it.

Decorative lights

4

- Pendants
- Ceiling-mounted fixtures
- Wall lights
- Floor-standing lamps
- Table lamps
- Desk lamps
- Kids' and fun lighting
- Picture lights
- Outdoor lights

The types of decorative lighting you choose for your home, rather like what you choose to wear, say more about you than any other part of your lighting scheme. A decorative light fixture is designed to be seen. Unlike architectural lighting—which is at its best when it remains unseen, providing effect, atmosphere and practical levels of light—the introduction of a decorative light fixture to a space has a major visual impact. Like the colors you choose for your walls or your choice of furniture and other fixtures, this is a chance for you to add your personal stamp to your home.

Pendants Classic

A classic pendant will always be a great investment, and you can install one of these timeless designs in most schemes. Clean lines, natural tones and simplicity of concept characterize classic pendants, and this makes it easy to choose a fixture that will look stylish. A great bonus of this type of fixture is that it is unlikely to look outdated, even when styles change.

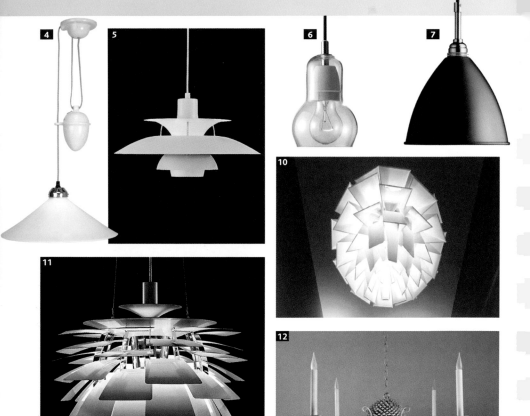

1 Titan
A design from the 1940s that is available in a variety of finishes. By Original BTC.

2 Large longlight
With a large ivory silk shade, this light comes with a drop rod in either polished nickel or satin nickel. By CTO Lighting.

3 Pendant bowl
The simplicity of this zinc fixture makes it suitable for both modern and traditional interiors. By Besselink and Jones.

4 Cobb rise and fall
Adjustable rise and fall pendant, ideal over dining tables and in kitchens. With bone china rose and shade. By Original BTC.

5 PH 50
Provides glare-free lighting for hanging above a table; 1958 design by Poul Henningsen. By Louis Poulsen.

6 Bulb pendant lamp
The lamp shade, bulb and even the wire are transparent. The reflective quality and thickness of the mouth-blown glass give the bulb lamp life—a real strength of good glass art. By Unique Copenhagen.

7 Bestlite pendant lamp
This lamp is based on a 1930 design by Robert Dudley Best that was hugely successful as the first British example of a Bauhaus product. By Bestlite.

8 Sorbonne
Glass crystal chandelier with four lights. By Vaughan.

9 1900 lantern
In black bronze and nickel, this lamp is also available in a variety of different metal and paint finishes and comes with faceted glass as standard. By Charles Edwards.

10 Norm 69 shade
Designed in 1969 by Simon Karko, this has become a Scandinavian design classic, striking in daylight and dramatic when lit. By the Conran Shop.

11 Artichoke lamp
Designed more than 40 years ago, this masterpiece, with a stainless-steel finish, has 72 leaves in 12 circular rows. This design allows the fixture to be viewed from any angle without exposing the light source located in the center. Designed by Poul Henningsen for Louis Poulsen.

12 Pinecone chandelier
This four-branched chandelier is a timeless design. By Porta Romana.

13 Light drizzle chandelier
This design consists of a polished nickel frame with two tiers of clear glass drops or a black frame with black glass drops. By Ochre Lighting.

Pendants Contemporary

Often simple in design, a contemporary hanging pendant will be the first thing someone sees when they walk into a space. Some pieces are best hung on their own, whereas smaller fixtures can be grouped and hung at different heights over kitchen islands or coffee tables.

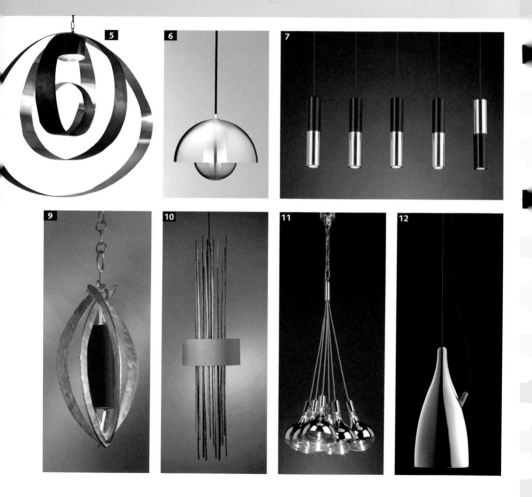

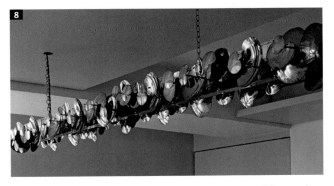

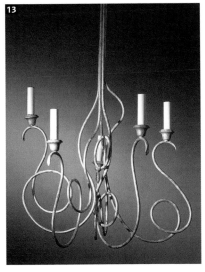

Featured designs

1 Turbo
Hanging light composed of 12 identical white-sprayed aluminum spiral-shaped segments; 1965 design by Louis Weisdorf. By Lyfa.

2 Aero
A slate-gray silk design embellished with hand-blown glass balls. By CTO Lighting.

3 Circle line
A drop pendant with a painted bone-china shade. By Original BTC.

4 Magnum 4202
Also available in black and in white. By Secto Design.

5 Lunar
A halogen pendant with an antique-bronze and satin-brass finish. By CTO Lighting.

6 Flowerpot pendant
Designed by Verner Panton in 1969, this is a polished aluminum pendant that is available in several colors. By Unique Copenhagen.

7 Baton pendant lamp
This design by Jos Muller is made of anodized-black and polished aluminum. By Quasar.

8 Eucalyptus
Thirty-eight extra-long LED lights on a patinated brass or pewter frame. By Ochre Lighting.

9 Miro
This pendant has a bright gold finish and comes with a silk shade. By Porta Romana.

10 Flynn stairwell lantern
Composed of vertical gold rods within a pearl silk shade. By Porta Romana.

11 Helios
Designed by Rob Nollet, this is a cluster of spotlight-style bulbs in stainless steel with polished aluminum. By Quasar.

12 Rorrim
This small pendant is made from heatproof glass. By Yamagiwa.

13 Medusa
Available in white gold. By Porta Romana.

14 UFO
This energy-efficient fixture has a central glass diffuser surrounded by 36 outer diffusers in a variety of colors. By Studio Italia Design.

Pendants Contemporary continued

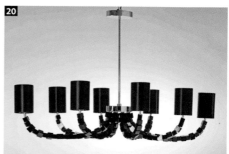

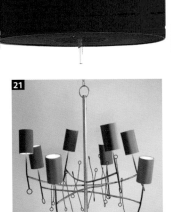

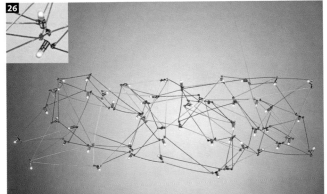

Featured designs

15 Collage 450
This three-tiered design in laser-cut acrylic provides a delicate play of light. By Louise Campbell.

16 Big Bang
Designed by Enrico Franzolini, this design is made of intersecting panels and incorporates a halogen bulb. By Foscarini.

17 Polo
Also available in ivory, dove gray and black silk. By CTO Lighting.

18 Drum shade light
Pictured in nickel, this striking fixture is available in several finishes. By Charles Edwards.

19 Tolomeo mega suspension light
Aluminum and injection-molded transparent methacrylate. Designed by Michele de Lucchi in 2007. By Artemide.

20 Lartigue
Cylindrical silk shades are incorporated into this oval black glass chandelier. By Porta Romana.

21 Lollipop chandelier
Scratched gold fixture with gold-lined, slate blue silk shades. By Porta Romana.

22 Crystal drop chandelier
A contemporary interpretation of a traditional chandelier. By Vaughan.

23 Koshi M pendant light
Dark bamboo shades with blown-glass satin white diffuser and chrome-plated fixtures. Designed by Manuel Vivian. By Axo Light.

24 Butterfly ball
Composed of 176 porcelain butterflies, which appear to be swarming around the central light source. By Diffuse.

25 Colored crystal chandelier
Long pendant dining-table light available in different lengths. Designed by Otto Cento. By Inspired by Design.

26 Universe
Designed by Jan Pauwels; available in brass or nickel. By Quasar.

Pendants Traditional

The traditional combination of glass and metal in a beautifully designed object is hard to beat. The play of light on a chandelier exudes a glamorous and sophisticated feel, and such fixtures sit well over dining tables and in entrance hallways. When located in a deep bay window, they extend the sense of space.

Featured designs

1 Shadow ball
In antique silver or brass. By Vaughan.

2 Art deco design
A 1925 French design. Wrought iron with scrolled-glass shades.

3 Fontana Murano chandelier
Italian glass chandelier. By Barovier & Toso.

4 Art nouveau pendant
An early 20th-century design. This three-arm pendant has a brass finish with scrolls and glass shades with teardrops.

5 Arts and crafts lantern pendant
This metal lantern design has pierced decoration and a frosted-glass shade.

6 Edwardian-style pendant
A polished-brass pendant light with a white satin glass bowl edged with brass rope detail.

7 Perry-style chandelier
This reproduction of a period-style chandelier has 16 lights on two tiers. By Wilkinson.

8 Rain drop chandelier
Incorporating Swarovsky crystals, this design is available in a variety of finishes. By Valerie Wade.

9 Modernist chandelier
This 1960s design by Sciolari in polished chrome and satin brass has a clear glass shade with candle bulbs.

10 Menton
This fixture has a nickel outer structure that can be lined with a fabric of your choice. By Vaughan.

11 Glass disc chandelier
Made from clear and black Murano glass; available with six, eight or ten lights. By Bella Figura.

12 Winslow
A square four-light lantern in brass. By Vaughan.

13 Flemish-style chandelier
Pictured here is a model with 15 lights on two tiers; a three-tier version with 24 lights is also available. By Wilkinson.

14 Regency-style chandelier
This "tent and waterfall" design is typical of the early 1800s. By Wilkinson.

15 Thornham Hall chandelier
A reproduction of one of the earliest surviving examples of an English Georgian lead-crystal chandelier. The original fixture made for Thornham Hall in Suffolk in 1732, now hangs at Winterthur, Delaware. By Wilkinson.

Ceiling-mounted fixtures

Where the ceiling is low or where there is no opportunity to recess lights, a ceiling-mounted fixture can provide a solution, especially in vestibules and hallways. The demand for such lights has lead designers to create some superb fixtures that would not look out of place in a living room. Choose a design that will shed light all around the fixture.

1 Artichoke
This is a flush-fitting version of a classic design. By Vaughan.

2 Silver bowl
This period-style fixture is made from antique silver and glass. By Vaughan.

3 Glass-beaded fixture
Designed by Emma Pi. By Inspired by Design.

4 Caboche
Designed by Patricia Urquiola. Transparent globes with a Murano glass diffuser are the key elements of this fixture. By Foscarini.

5 Crown
This flush-fitting ceiling light in antique brass is available in a range of other finishes. By Hector Finch.

6 Presidio oval
A design by Barbara Barry in satin nickel. By Boyd Lighting.

7 Palos verdes
A satin aluminum ceiling light designed by Barbara Barry. By Boyd Lighting.

8 Rouen
A looped-glass design. By Vaughan.

9 Octagonal ceiling light
This brushed-nickel design incorporates four bulbs. By Vaughan.

10 Circolo
Designed by Doyle Crosby, this ceiling light incorporates four bulbs. By Boyd Lighting.

11 Planar
A bathroom ceiling light in a frosted finish. By Astro Lighting.

12 Miami
A bathroom ceiling light in a brushed aluminum finish. By Astro Lighting.

13 Duplex
This bathroom ceiling light comes in a frosted finish. By Astro Lighting.

14 Taketa
A bathroom ceiling light in a matte nickel finish. By Astro Lighting.

15 Bulkhead light
A die-cast rectangular bulkhead light with curved frosted glass diffuser. By Davey Lighting.

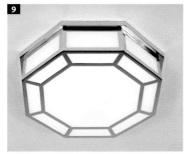

Wall lights Contemporary

The huge choice of contemporary-style wall fixtures now available can make it difficult to pinpoint which design is right for your space. There are no rules, except to choose something aesthetically appealing to you. A contemporary-style wall light should be noticeable, rather like a piece of art, so don't be afraid to make a bold choice. Always try to see the fixture illuminated before you buy.

Featured designs

1 Array triple
This three-lamp fixture is in antique bronze and has a satin-brass base and black cotton shades with gold lining. By CTO Lighting.

2 Charlie
This fixture has a frame in brushed nickel and a diffuser in white hand-blown glass or perforated metal. By Studio Italia.

3 Pompeii wall light
Shown with an ivory linen lamp shade and in a nickel finish. Also available in a gold finish. By Vaughan.

4 Fields wall light
A modular wall lamp composed of three elements that can be installed either individually or in combination. Made of methacrylic and aluminum. By Foscarini.

5 Flynn wall light
A fixture created from gold-colored latticed metal with a semi-circular putty-colored silk shade. By Porta Romana.

6 Secto 4230
Pleated-look wall lamp. By Secto.

7 Blossom
Wall light with glass detail in white gold and an oval, open-back putty-colored silk shade. By Porta Romana:

8 Icicle
A bathroom wall light with a silk shade. By Porta Romana.

9 Square wall light
By AXO Light.

10 Andrei
Designed by Brian Rasmussen in 2008, this wall light has a metal frame and is available in white or mirror-finished polished stainless steel. By Studio Italia.

11 Catacaos
A slim fixture that can be mounted vertically or horizontally. Designed by Federico Otero. By Boyd Lighting.

12 Twig
Two-arm asymmetrical wall light with white card half lamp shades. By Vaughan.

13 Lollipop
A two-arm brushed-gold fixture with cylindrical satin shades. By Porta Romana.

14 Double 07
Wall light with support in lacquered metal and a glass diffuser that is white inside with white or ivory outer finish. By Foscarini.

15 Eucalyptus
This fixture has patinated brass or pewter frames and is available with either five or two LED lights. By Ochre Lighting.

16 Arctic pear
Patinated bronze on nickel frame with two tiers of solid glass drops. By Ochre Lighting.

17 Glass-beaded wall light
By Boyd Lighting.

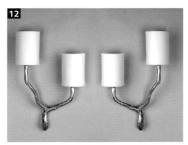

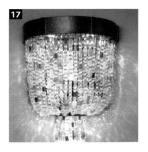

Wall lights Classic/Traditional

Classic wall lights fit well into all types of interiors; their simple lines and neutral tones will blend easily into most decorative schemes. Often finished in polished brass and dark antique bronze, traditional wall lights slip into period-style rooms and create pockets of warm light. They work best where ceilings are low.

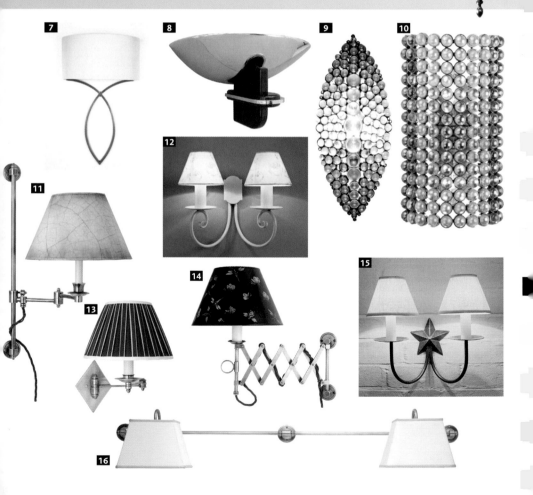

Featured designs

1 Torch-style wall sconces
These 1940s French sconces feature the original frozen-flame frosted-glass shades. By Decodame.

2 Lead crystal wall chandelier
An elegant design of classic crystal drops. By Period Style Lighting.

3 Georgian-style wall light
Brass wall light. By Period Style Lighting.

4 & 5 Brooke/Lameia
Victorian-style down- and up-lights. The Brook has a hand-cut pineapple glass shade. The Lameia's glass shade is hand-blown. By Period Style Lighting.

6 Austin wall light
Arts and crafts-style black metal sconce with frosted glass shade. By Rejuvenation.

7 Art deco wall sconce
A 21st-century mahogany sconce with crossed "tusk" design. By Decodame.

8 Walter Prosper Art Deco wall sconce
Thick, sculpted black Lucite forms a modern deco design. By Decodame.

9 Sea pod
This lozenge-shaped wall light was designed by Emily Todhunter. By Best and Lloyd.

10 Beluga wall
This fixture diffuses warm light through its crescent-shaped glass shade.

11 Library light
Adjustable two-arm light. By Besselink and Jones.

12 Scrolled wall light
This wall light in old gold has a cream trim and silk shade. By Jim Lawrence.

13 Marilyn Monroe
Distressed brass fixture with feminine shade. By Besselink and Jones.

14 Lazy Doris
This wall light in distressed brass can be folded away. By Besselink and Jones.

15 Star
This solid brass double wall light in old gold has a star motif. By Jim Lawrence.

16 Double picture light
This double horizontal picture light in distressed brass illuminates a large area. By Besselink and Jones.

17 Tall drum wall light
Made up of nine suspended porcelain tiles. By Diffuse.

18 Morton
Hurricane-style lamp. By Jim Lawrence.

19 Scallop shell
Plaster wall light. By Porta Romana.

20 Ombrelle
This French-style design incorporates a ceramic shade. By Hector Finch.

21 Deco
This art deco wall light is made from satin brass or satin nickel. By CTO Lighting.

22 Portofino
A chrome light that is ideal for bathrooms. By Best and Lloyd.

Floor-standing lamps Classic and traditional

A classic floor-standing light is often important as an essential element in a lighting scheme. Use the quirky charm of an oversized version of a classic fixture to create a focal point, as well as to supply essential practical light. A traditional-style floor-standing lamp will blend in with a period interior.

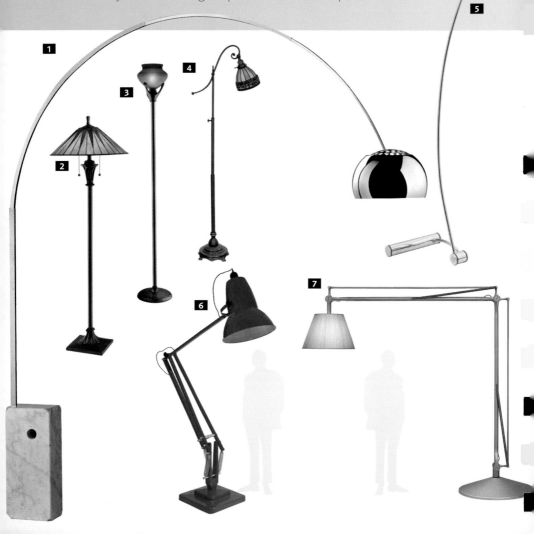

Featured designs

1 Marble-based floor lamp
Designed by Achille Castiglioni and Pier Giacomo Castiglioni, this 1962 lamp features a telescopic steel stem and a swivel joint at the base. By Flos.

2 Gotham
In the style of Tiffany, this floor lamp has hand-cut art-glass panels on the shade that send a warm glow upward, outward and below. By Quoizel.

3 Beaux-Arts torchiere
This floor light comes with a three-way switch and an amber orange seeded-glass torchiere shade with hundreds of tiny air bubbles that provide a warm, textured look. By Quoizel.

4 Pomez agate
This handcrafted art-glass shade features genuine hand-polished agate stones. By Quoizel.

5 Arc
Almost a sculpture, this floor light provides a soft light and was designed by an Italian pupil of Frank Lloyd Wright. By Best and Lloyd.

6 Anglepoise Giant 1227
Three times the size of the desk lamp, this classic has aluminum casters for easy positioning and comes with a bulb and dimmer. By Anglepoise.

7 Superarchimoon
Designed by Philippe Starck and based on his original desk light design, this floor light is now a classic. By Flos.

8 Swing-arm floor lamp
The swing arm makes it unnecessary to move this floor lamp around for different tasks. By Bella Figura.

9 Pimlico tripod
This floor light is available in three metallic finishes. By Artemis Design.

10 Smartie major
Claw feet in brushed nickel make this standard floor lamp ideal for a traditional space. By Besselink and Jones.

11 Nora floor lamp
Part of the Emily Todhunter collection. By Best & Lloyd.

12 Victor
This elegant floor lamp has a shade in satin-painted aluminum, a base in polished aluminum and a support stem in chromed steel. By Original BTC.

13 Adjustable floor lamp
Adjusted via an arm, this is a versatile and easy-to-maneuver lamp. By Bella Figura.

14 Angle floor lamp
Suited to light a range of tasks, this floor lamp is elegant as well as functional. By Bella Figura.

15 Elevator floor lamp
These sculptural and versatile floor lamps designed by Pii are fitted with a dimmer. By Quasar.

Floor-standing lamps Contemporary

Fun and easy to use, the contemporary plug-in floor-standing light is an affordable way to achieve instant style in any room. Their portability ensures that any investment is one for life, as you can always take it with you if you move. Use these experimental styles to inject color into any space. An understated contemporary piece will introduce calmness to your scheme.

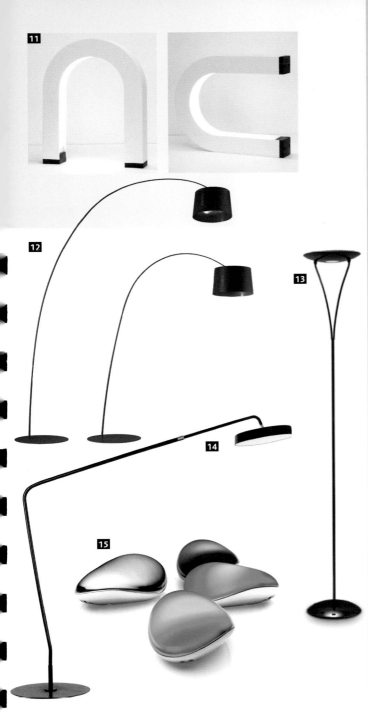

Featured designs

1&2 Tag/Azumi floor lights
Polished nickel finish floor lamps designed by Astro Lighting.

3 Ghost
This lamp, designed by Gitta Geschwendtner, has a polished nickel base. By CTO Lighting.

4 Halo
The clean lines of the polished nickel base are complemented by a dove gray or black silk shade. By CTO Lighting.

5 Axis mundi
This design is distinguished by a solid glass rod set into a polished nickel base and a soft silk-lined diagonal pleated and laminated silk or card shade. By Ochre Lighting.

6 Beam lights
Blown glass and spun aluminum shade. By Industrial Facility/Sam Hecht.

7 Tolomeo floor light
A polished aluminum light designed by Michele de Lucchi and Giancarlo Fassina. By Artemide.

8 Tolomeo Mega Terra
A design by Michele de Lucchi and Giancarlo Fassina with cantilevered structure in polished aluminum. By Artemide.

9 Lucifer
Designed by Wever & Ducré.

10 Metta
This lamp has a solid wood base with an ivory cotton shade. By CTO Lighting.

11 White structured lamp
An arresting sculptural lamp. By Wever & Ducré.

12 Twiggy
A design by Marc Sadler with a lacquered glass fiber flat base that is weighted to provide alternative heights. By Foscarini.

13 Opus
This halogen uplight has an opening in the base of the shade that provides downward diffusion. By ML.

14 Reach
This lamp has a satin black base and opal diffuser. By CTO Lighting.

15 Aduki light
Color-changing rechargeable light shaped like a metallic bean. By Mathmos.

Table lamps Classic

A classic table lamp is a great source of essential warm light. It is worth investing in the best examples you can afford, as table lamps are right in your eye line. Size matters—the larger the lamp, the greater the amount of light produced. Where there is restricted space, such as in a narrow hallway, you will gain a similar advantage by choosing a tall, rather than a squat, style.

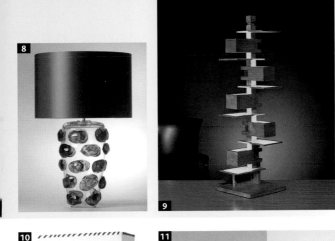

Featured designs

1 Bauhaus glass base lamp
This table lamp is a replica of that designed by Wilhelm Wagenfeld in 1924. Referred to as the Bauhaus lamp, the base and rod are made of glass and the finishings of polished chrome steel.

2 Grenoble
Crystal lamp with a black silk drum lampshade. By Vaughan.

3 Tullamore crystal lamp
A solid crystal ballustrade lamp designed by Sandy Chapman. Externally wired with clear cable so as not to interfere with the classic design.

4 Jules
Table lamp. By Best and Lloyd.

5 Pisa table lamp
The angled base of this lamp is available in bronze, brass and nickel finishes. By Vaughan.

6 Fleur
Large antique silver-leaf lamp with a rectangular black silk shade (shown with silver lining). By Heathfield.

7 Polo
Round Plexiglas lamp with oval brown silk shade. By Porta Romana.

8 Glass blob lamp
Available in several colors, this lamp comes with a cylinder satin shade in a matching color. By Porta Romana.

9 Taliesin
Designed by Frank Lloyd Wright in cherry wood and one of a series of three. By Yamagiwa.

10 Distressed brass stand
Slim double-stem table lamp in distressed brass. By Besselink and Jones.

11 Atollo
With a shade that appears to almost hover in midair, this classic 1977 design is by Vico Magistretti. By Oluce.

12 Lartigue crystal cubes
A cylindrical taupe silk shade complements this simple design of stacked cubes. By Porta Romana.

13 Doma
A wonderfully elegant Art Deco shape reminiscent of 1930s hotels and cruise ships. When lit, the translucent shade glows warmly, giving a broad spread of diffused as well as direct light. By BTC.

14 Medium Adam lamp
Stacked glass pebbles in different sizes. By Porta Romana.

Table lamps Contemporary

Rather like a piece of sculpture, contemporary table lamps will always make a big visual impact. Careful positioning is key. It is worth considering both the light source and how much ambient light, as opposed to direct light, it sheds. Any glare will draw the eye for all the wrong reasons. Use color-injected glass, Plexiglas or even card fittings to create useful pockets of light. Metal disks add glamour and shimmer and will cast fabulous shadows.

Featured designs

1 Crystal vase base
Utrecht crystal vase base with brass fittings, shown here with a black linen shade. By Vaughn.

2 Alfie lamp
Pictured in turquoise and in gold and red with shades in different colorways. By William Yeoward.

3 Hand-blown glass
French hand-blown bottle base. By La-Lou.

4 Cherub lamp
Hand-blown glass base in smoked amethyst, with polished nickel fittings and a silk shade. By Ochre Lighting.

5 Glass lava lamp
A transparent green glass base with a dove satin shade. By Porta Romana.

6 Coffee bean glass lamp
Bronze-colored glass base with a straight oval-shaped, taupe silk shade. By Porta Romana.

7 Deco
Satin-brass or satin-nickel base with a dove gray or black silk shade. By CTO Lighting.

8 Tate table lamp
This design recalls the paintings of Piet Mondrian. By Best and Lloyd.

9 Large anemone
This organic design is by Emily Todhunter. By Best and Lloyd.

10 Mirrored ball
Designed by Emily Todhunter. By Best and Lloyd.

11 Olive ball
Emily Todhunter designed this tactile globe-shaped lamp. By Best and Lloyd.

12 Cardin
This sumptuous mirrored design is by Anthony Critchlow. By Best and Lloyd.

Table lamps Contemporary continued

13

14

15

16

17

18

19

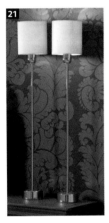

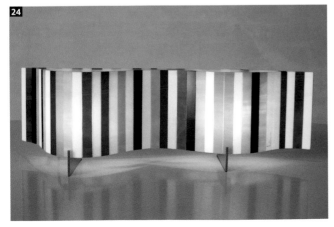

Featured designs

13 Blow
Designed by Pio E Tito Toso in 2005. The light source can be adjusted from the outside through a magnet placed on the diffuser. By Studio Italia.

14 Z Lamp
Distressed brass base with a square shade. By Besselink and Jones.

15 Crystal strata lamp
Coal-nickel base with rectangular platinum silk shade. By Porta Romana.

16 Rectangular lamp
Striking rectangular lamp with a putty-colored silk shade. By Porta Romana.

17 Glamour
Like a unique piece of jewelry for the home, Glamour's rows of individually hand-soldered metal links recall a necklace. By Terzani.

18 PXL table lamp
Made in aluminum and steel, this multicolored design is by Fredrik Mattsson. By Zero.

19 Marie-Louise table light
Made in acrylic and polycarbonate. By Sander Mulder.

20 Paradise table lamp
Part of the Retro Murano Collection, this design comes in glass finishes, including milk white and crystal, plus 24-carat gold and metal finishes, including chrome and gold. By Bella Figura.

21 Piccolo round
Silk ivory shade on a slender base. By Heathfield.

22 Red ball table lamp
A red ball table lamp in resin complete with tall silk drum shade. By Tindle Lighting.

23 Tribal lamp
Inspired by a Sumatran tribal necklace. By La-Lou.

24 Vento pop
Table lamp with glass glued on methacrylate. By Arturo Alvarez.

Table lamps Traditional

The coolie-style shade is the most popular choice for traditional table lamps. The coolie shade sits well on even the most decorative lamp base, but it is worth branching out from the standard cream-colored shade. Not only does a cream silk allow the hot spot of the light source to be seen, but it will give a cool light. Try gold-lined, dark shades, which give a more atmospheric light.

Featured designs

1 Original gas lamp
Original gas lamps are available from vintage stores.

2 Bungalow table lamp
In the style of Tiffany, this lamp is an arts and crafts design. By Quoizel.

3 Green dragonfly table lamp
This reproduction is based on an original Tiffany design attributed to Clara Driscoll, one of the studio's first female artisans. By Quoizel.

4 Glenhaven
This art nouveau–style lamp has a thick etched-glass shade in swirled brown and amber. By Robert Abby Inc.

5 Azoricum
This handmade Tiffany-style glass table lamp has a solid brass base. By Period Style Lighting.

6 The Cornelia
This lamp, in the French art nouveau style, has a hand-blown frosted-glass shade and hand-etched purple flowers. By Period Style Lighting.

7 French art deco table lamp
The statue design for this table lamp dates from 1920. By Decodame.

8 Art deco table lamp
Copper table lamp by Artemis Design.

9 Astro C
Inspired by the industrial desk lamps of the 1940s, this Robert Abbey lamp, finished in brushed chrome, has a metal push-button dimmer switch built into the base. By Robert Abby Inc.

10 French art deco table lamp
Made in France in the 1920s, this lamp's molded glass shade is supported by a wrought-iron base. By Decodame.

11 Art deco double-arm table candelabra
This elegant art deco table lamp, with a nickel-plated double-arm base, was made in Paris in the 1930s. By Decodame.

12 Corn-on-the-cob table lamp
Made in France in the mid-20th century, this table lamp features a brushed-steel base. By Decodame.

13 Hexagon
This lamp has a glass coolie shade and a solid brass base with a bronze finish. By The English Lamp Company.

14 Trafalgar
With a heavy square base in solid brass, this is a classic column table lamp. By The English Lamp Company.

15 Ceramic jar table lamp
The ceramic hand-painted jar base incorporates the Chinese Double Happiness symbol. By Orchid.

16 Temple jar table lamp
This blue and white temple jar has a gilded base. By Besselink and Jones.

17 Tea caddy lamp
The painted base of this lamp is inspired by a traditional tea caddy design. By Besselink and Jones.

Desk lamps

Ensure that any desk lamp you choose actually does provide useful light. Cantilevered designs are good for directing light where it is needed. For a tight space, you may consider a wall-mounted option. Developments in LED have seen a huge rise in the number of cutting-edge desk lamps. Opting for such a fixture is an easy way to make a bold design statement.

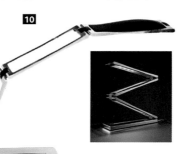

Featured designs

1 Dove table lamp
An elegant table lamp with a built-in double intensity switch. Designed by Mario Barbaglia and Marco Colombo.

2 Prototype table lamp
Designed by Bernhard Dessecker and Ingo Maurer in 2001, this lamp is made in aluminum, stainless steel, brass, plastic and silicon.

3 Bill table lamp
A classic two-armed articulated lamp, this fixture is highly flexible and easy to adjust. By Tobias Grau.

4 Little BIG Lamp
A steel, aluminum, glass and plastic lamp, designed by Ingo Maurer.

5 Table light
This slim-line light was designed by Tobias Grau.

6 Tizio 50
This design in black or chrome is by Richard Sapper.

7 Twiggy table lamp
This lamp, made from compound material on a lacquered glass fiber base, was designed by Marc Sadler. By Foscarini.

8 Tolomeo table light
Designed by Michele de Lucchi and Giancarlo Fassina in silver polished and anodized aluminum.

9 Melampo bedside
This lamp, with a gray or bronze painted aluminum base and satin-silk and plastic shade, was designed by Adrien Gardere.

10 Chain LED
Designed by Ilaria Marelli, this versatile folding table lamp is made of polished or pearl white aluminum.

11 Anglepoise
The original 1227 table light, designed by George Carwardine, was reissued to celebrate its 75th anniversary and is made with aluminum arms and a heavily weighted base for extra stability. By Anglepoise.

12 Bauhaus table lamp
A copy of a lamp originally designed by Eduard Wilifred Buquet in 1927. Various versions were produced until the 1940s.

13 Traditional brass bankers' light
Reproductions of this classic 19th-century design remain a popular choice for traditional interiors. By Besselink & Jones.

14 Halogen bankers' light
Design with a brass stand. Also available in bronze, chrome and nickel finishes. By Besselink & Jones.

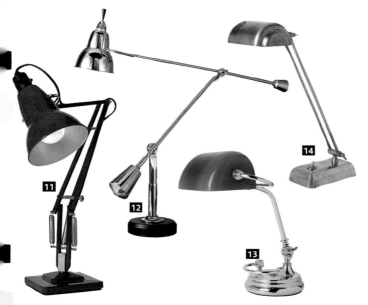

Kids' and fun lighting

You can make a child's space appealing simply by fitting a colored shade on a central pendant. Wall-mounted reading lights in the shape of an animal will provide practical as well as fun light fixtures. Alternatively, consider opting for pretty bunches of suspended glass to act as bedside lights, or drape strings of lights around the room.

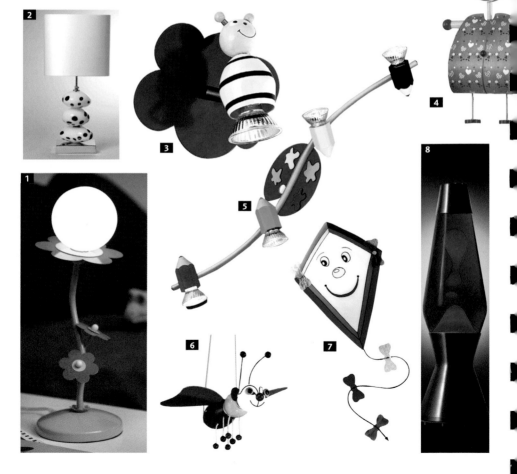

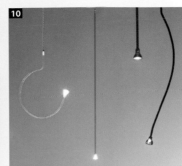

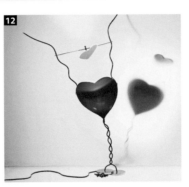

Featured designs

1 Flower table lamp
A multicolored children's table lamp. Also available as wall and ceiling lights. By Eglo.

2 Dalmatian
This is a light-hearted variant of the small Adam lamp design. By Porta Romana.

3 Bee wall light
This children's wall light is designed by Eglo.

4 Boy/Girl ceiling light
A children's pendant ceiling light available in a pink or blue finish. By Eglo.

5 Spotlight wall/ceiling light
This colorful four-spot light can be used either as a wall or ceiling light. Also available with two spotlights. By Eglo.

6 Susi bee wall light
A wood and synthetic ceiling pendant. By Eglo.

7 Jeff–Smiley kite
This light for a children's room is available as a wall or ceiling fixture. By Eglo.

8 Astro lava lamp
Handmade in the U.K. since 1963, the first and original lava lamp was designed by Edward Craven-Walker, who invented it by adapting a design for an egg-timer. By Mathmos.

9 Galaverna
Glass pendant lights designed by Pepe Tanzi.

10 Fili'Angelo
Glass pendant lights designed by Pepe Tanzi. By Album.

11 Wish upon a star
Hand-painted bone-china shade. By Original BTC.

12 From the heart
Designed by Ingo Maurer in 1989, this table lamp is made of metal and plastic with an adjustable glass mirror.

13 Orbital
This floor lamp, designed by Ferruccio Laviani in 1992, is constructed of colored or white silkscreen-printed glass plates in various shapes mounted onto a lacquer structure.

14 Farfalla
These glass lights were designed by Pepe Tanzi. By Album.

15 Bulb table lamp
A larger-than-life glass lamp. By Ingo Maurer.

Picture lights

The atmosphere that a picture light introduces to a room is invaluable. Always choose the source carefully, depending on the item to be lit; a dense oil painting can take a good punch of light, whereas a watercolor or drawing needs a more delicate touch. Be aware of any glare or reflections from glass-fronted paintings, and always consider the size of the item before choosing the most suitable fixture. If in doubt, seek advice from a lighting designer.

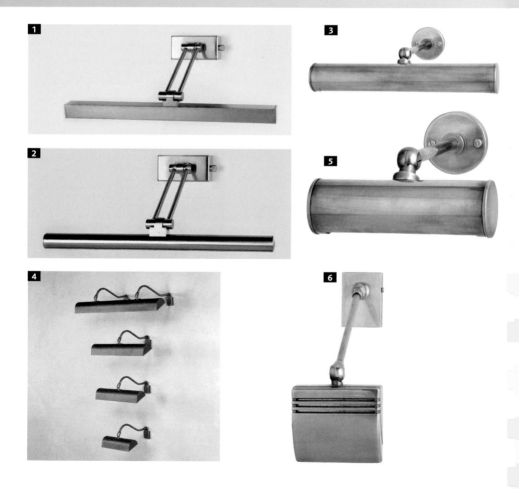

1 & 2 Square/Round profile
A square-profile adjustable picture light in nickel. By Porta Romana.

3 Brass picture light (small)
A traditional distressed-brass design. By Besselink and Jones.

4 Swan neck
This design is available in a range of sizes. By Vaughan.

5 Brass picture light (large)
A traditional distressed-brass design. By Besselink and Jones.

6 Arrow wall light
By Besselink and Jones.

7 Academy light
This light can be customized to the specific requirements of individual paintings and works of art. By Precision Lighting.

8 & 9 Pictura Contemporary/Traditional
The frosted halogen bulbs in these low-voltage picture lights softens light distribution. By John Cullen Lighting.

10 Antique traditional
This standard-voltage picture light can be fixed directly to the wall or frame. By John Cullen Lighting.

11 Flexilight
A flexible low-voltage contemporary picture light that is suitable for lighting pictures and objects or for mounting on the ceiling. By John Cullen Lighting.

12 Framing projector
The beam of this fully concealed projector, can be controlled to frame paintings or objects of any shape. By John Cullen Lighting.

13 Phantasia
The arm of this flexible contemporary low-voltage picture light is fixed directly to the wall, lighting the picture with a single bulb. By John Cullen Lighting.

14 Phantamount
This discreet display light, designed to fit on top of display panels or picture frames, is available in brushed aluminum with either curved or straight rods. By Precision Lighting.

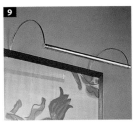

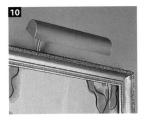

Outdoor lights

A properly lit external space will extend the boundaries of a home. The availability of a huge range of weatherproof fixtures means that there are lots of lighting options to choose from. The variety of traditional-style wall lanterns and porch lights is now complemented by freestanding garden lights. Moreover, you can now go for splashes of color with LEDs.

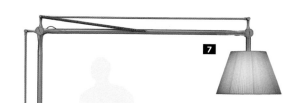

Featured designs

1 Deck light
Available in either dark green painted or weathered finish and either clear or opal glass. By Davey Lighting.

2 Gina
A lantern in nickel. By Charles Edwards.

3 Regency pineapple lantern
This hanging lantern is in faux zinc. By Charles Edwards.

4 Gatepost lantern
This tapering French-style lantern is in charcoal-colored paint with brass detail. By Charles Edwards.

5 French porch lantern
This bronze and nickel design is a modern reproduction of a traditional style. By Charles Edwards.

6 French wall lantern
This pewter lantern is shown with a reservoir and frosted-glass tube. By Charles Edwards.

7 Romeo lighting in the rain
This floor light is from a family of outdoor lights designed by Philippe Starck. By Flos.

8 Brass bulkhead light
Die-cast in natural brass with frosted glass diffuser. By Davey Lighting.

9 Box wall lantern
The frosted glass on this fixture produces a soft light. By John Cullen Lighting.

10 Footliter
This spiked fixture provides low-level ground lighting. By John Cullen Lighting.

11 Alexander wall lantern
This fixture incorporates an energy-efficient LED. By John Cullen Lighting.

12 L'uovo
By Yamagiwa.

13 Kanipazar garden light
By B.lux.

14 Imperial wall lantern
This 10-finned wall sconce is available in different sizes. By Boyd Lighting.

15 Colored floor lights
By Bloempot.

16 Havana outdoor lamp
This stake-mounted lamp has a diffuser made of molded polythene and a metal support. By Foscarini.

17 Pendant light
A design by Louis Poulsen.

18 Passage
A pendant light designed by Kevin Reilly.

19 Clipper Light
This neat wall light is finished in antiqued brass. By Jim Lawrence.

20 Spinaker
This low-voltage feature light is suitable for lighting down walls and providing pools of light. By John Cullen Lighting.

21 Odeon
A nickel wall lantern. By Charles Edwards.

22 Exterior floor lights
By Oluce.

- Front doors and porches
- Entrances and hallways
- Stairs and landings
- Living rooms
- Kitchens

In the home

PART 5

- Dining rooms
- Open-plan living
- Children's rooms
- Home offices
- Wine cellars
- Media rooms
- Half baths
- Bedrooms
- Bathrooms
- Home gyms
- Swimming pools
- Sunrooms
- Outdoor spaces
- Details

This section will show you how lighting can enhance every room in your home, using both architectural and decorative lighting tools to create flexible, beautiful, functional and dramatic spaces. Good lighting can revolutionize a space. It creates mood and can open up or close down spaces at the touch of a button. A thoughtful lighting scheme provides a backdrop that will showcase interior design, highlight artwork, link internal and external spaces, facilitate the flexible use of open-plan spaces, provide practical lighting in the home office or kitchen and give soft, ambient light for relaxed socializing.

Front doors and porches

The front door to your home is the first thing visitors see, and improving the lighting at your front door is a great way of creating a stylish and welcoming impression while providing practical light for you and your guests.

Apply the same rules of good lighting for the inside of a house to the lighting outside a house. Review the space and think about which features you want to light and where you can best position the lighting. The external architecture of a house will dictate what will work best.

To make sure the entrance is lit even when you are out but without wasting energy during the day, it is worth considering wiring external lighting to a photocell. This is a simple piece of equipment that ensures the light is switched off during daylight hours. For security you may choose to add a motion

▲ **Elegant frame**
The warm light that cascades from this thoughtfully positioned pair of exterior wall lights frames the door and creates a welcoming glow.

▶ Warm welcome
The lighting from within the hall and adjacent rooms of this house provides an overspill and creates a gentle glow of welcoming light outside. The up/down lights either side of the front door create shadows through the creeping plants on the wall.

▲ Compact simplicity
Contemporary up/down wall lights dramatically frame this front door. Set at the perfect height in relation to the proportions of the door, they cast pools of light below and highlight the architectural details above. The warm glow from the pendant in the entrance shines through the glass over the door, providing a warm welcome.

◀ Structural subtlety
The simplicity of the uplit facade of this modern home is all that is required to draw the eye along the path toward the front door.

detector, which will turn any lights on when you approach. You can also install a timer to regulate your external lighting so it operates at predetermined times.

Key tips
■ Consider the age of the property and the way similar houses nearby are lit. This will help you to decide what might best suit your house.

■ In a high-ceilinged porch, a hanging lantern can provide an attractive focus that will help to frame the front door and give off a soft, diffused light.

■ For a simple low porch, a basic waterproof low-voltage recessed spotlight will provide a clean, practical light.

■ Don't just stick to hanging or overhead lighting. For example, floor-recessed uplights will create a dramatic skim of light around a door.

■ Low-level floor washers are great for lighting a pathway.

■ LED step washers are a practical solution for lighting steps to the front door.

■ If there is glass on either side or on top of the front door, a hanging light in the entrance will shed additional warm light out onto a porch. Conversely, any lighting used outside risks creating glare in the entrance.

■ Consider ground-level recessed uplights to highlight architectural details for added drama.

■ Be careful to avoid positioning lights so that they highlight ugly features, such as drain pipes.

Entrances and hallways

The entrance can act as a decompression chamber from the outside world. Even if you don't spend a great deal of time in this space, it nevertheless has the essential function of creating a warm, welcoming atmosphere and sets the mood for the rest of your home.

▲ Dramatic entrance
A single low-voltage spotlight punches light over the floral arrangement to create dramatic shadows and an attractive focal point that draws the eye into the space.

Whatever the shape or size of your entrance, whether it is a narrow corridorlike space or a larger square or round space, your starting point should always be to create a welcoming atmosphere. It is also important to layer the light in the entrance, as you would in any other room, to provide depth and texture, particularly in smaller spaces.

You can create atmosphere by using standard-voltage light sources in wall lights, table lamps or hanging pendants, which will provide a warm yellow light. The simplest way to achieve this is to use a table lamp on a narrow console table or on a shelf over a radiator. In larger entrances, a pair of lamps will effectively frame a table with a picture or a mirror hung above it. It is always worthwhile to position sockets as discreetly as possible, for example, by installing them just below the height of the tabletop.

If you do not have room for a table lamp, standard-voltage wall lights or decorative picture lights can provide a space-saving alternative. Set at the right height, these provide that essential warm glow. Unless you have a large entrance, choose fixtures that

◀ **Welcome vista**
The uplights in the floor highlight the curved wall providing a focal point in the foreground. This is balanced by ceiling-recessed lights that highlight the artwork, which provide a strong pull for the eye. Low-level floor washers highlight the bright rug.

▼ **Eye-catching**
Three layers of light combine to make a spectacular impact in a very small space. Intermediate light glows from the wall, a low-level floor washer picks out the color and texture of the floor and a ceiling-recessed light provides a strong focus on the painting.

are shallow in depth or you risk making the entrance feel narrower than it actually is.

Pick out a focal point

Highlighting a focal point will help you to distract from the awkwardness of a difficult space. A focal point can be, for example, a picture or mirror on the wall, flowers on a console table or an object positioned on a landing that can be seen from the hallway. If you do not have a suitable focal point, a hanging standard-voltage decorative pendant is a great way to add visual "punctuation" to any size of entrance.

You can increase the apparent width of the space by using low-voltage directional recessed spots to bounce light off the walls. In addition, floor-recessed uplights are a great way to define archways or door frames. A word of warning however, avoid using a straight line of recessed downlights, which create a "runway" effect and light only the floor, as this will simply narrow the space.

You can combine several of these lighting options to create a layered effect. For example, a few low-level floor washers will highlight floor texture and color and draw your eye through the space. A table lamp perched on a radiator cover or on a narrow console table will add essential warmth, and low-voltage ceiling-recessed spotlights can wash the walls or light artwork or a mirror to create a sense of space. Place your different layers of light on separate circuits so you can use them at different times of day.

Key tips

■ Layer the light to give you flexibility, and ensure that each circuit is dimmable.

■ If you can use only one light source, use a standard-voltage incandescent bulb for warmth and atmosphere.

■ Use low-voltage directional spotlights to wash light onto the walls and give the impression of added width.

■ If using wall lights or picture lights, choose a slim design to avoid reducing the sense of space.

■ Use a decorative pendant light to provide visual interest if you lack a focal point.

◀ **Intermediate warmth**
The wall lights work well in this entrance hallway, setting a welcoming tone. The stair washers and window uplights provide focus and pick out highlights.

▶ **Structural engineering**
The simplicity of the lighting in this entrance creates a strong impact, making additional decoration redundant. The repetition of the low-voltage square downlights elongates the space. The height at which the fixtures are set — just short of the ceiling — allows them to sit effortlessly in the room.

◀ **Traditional focus**
In this entrance, wall lights are the foundation of a welcoming light. Floor-recessed uplights frame the space and draw you into it.

Stairs and landings

The stairs and landing of a home are essential connectors, and you should apply the same layered lighting strategy to these areas that you would apply to individual rooms. This ensures that stairs, landings and hallways are linked with the rest of the house. Thoughtfully positioned lighting controls will allow you to achieve the results you want with a minimum amount of clutter.

A key consideration is to avoid separating the hallway from the stairs in terms of the lighting. In many homes, the first floor landing can be seen from the entrance. It therefore makes sense to pay particular attention to how these areas are controlled.

Begin at a low level. Low-level floor washers are a practical as well as an understated way to light stairs of all types. LEDs are an expecially useful lighting solution for stairs because they are conveniently compact. Square or round fixtures recessed into the wall along a stair and set at a low level will gently skim light across the stair tread and lead the eye onward.

This form of lighting may not be suitable for use on stairs in the main parts of historic buildings, but they can often come into their own in older properties when used to light steps down to basements or cellars where no overhead lighting is possible. Low-level stair washers can also provide very useful night lighting. If you have an open banister, be sure that the lights are set low enough to not cause glare.

All in the detail
Under-cabinet lights in display cubes generate interest in the dead space of the half-landing. Lights wash the stairs and connect the lower and upper levels, and the eye is drawn upward by the wall light on the landing, which provides slim and unobtrusive atmospheric light.

◀ **Literary warmth**
This landing is brought to life with a discreet linear light source that softly washes the bookshelves. Cleverly, the architectural plaster wall light in this high-use area is fitted with an energy-efficient light source. Stair washers provide a useful night-light.

▲ **Light elevation**
Lit slots expand the sense of space in this narrow staircase, providing dramatic shadows and an architecturally unobtrusive light. The lighting on the stairs draws the eye up to the living room. The overall effect is calming and effortless.

Lighting restricted spaces

Another discreet way to introduce light into a restricted space, such as a stairway, is to insert a light source into the handrail. If you don't have a handrail, a simple slot set diagonally into the wall can be lit with a fluorescent tube to create a minimal but bold style statement as well as practical lighting.

If your staircase is open under the stairs, think about how you might light this space so it does not end up as a dead or blank hole. Linear standard-voltage rope light or an LED linear light source can be fixed to the underside of the edge of a stair to highlight the architectural line and add ambience to the space. Floor-recessed LED or standard-voltage uplights set close to the back wall will also add architectural definition and draw the eye further. Alternatively, adding an electrical socket will enable you to introduce a table lamp or a floor-based plug-in uplight behind an object to create light and shadows.

In narrow staircases, create slots or niches in one of the walls. Recess lights into the top or bottom of these slots to create a practical but dramatic light for your stairs that does not impinge on the space.

Window ledges on half-landings are also useful locations in which to recess uplights. Set close to a window frame, these will highlight the architectural details and provide dramatic light that can be seen from both inside and outside the building. LED uplights are a good choice. These are cool to the touch so that proximity to fabric (for example, drapes) is not a problem.

Even in the most limited spaces, you can often find room for a skinny low-voltage up/down light to frame a window on a half-landing, or you can use a plaster square-style

▲ Reflected glory
A textured pendant is reflected in the arched mirror, pulling the eye up to the landing and giving depth to the hallway. Stair washers provide an elegant progression toward the uplit arch.

▶ Open view
The open treads invite the eye to travel beyond to the lit area under the stairs (inset), where inground uplights gently wash up the wall and provide background lighting to the chairs placed in the otherwise dead space. The stair washers bring out the color and texture of the wooden treads.

◄ Unimpeded space
The space in this tightly winding staircase is unimpeded by the series of low-voltage square lights. The contemporary design of the wall lights blends well with the traditional wooden banister.

up/down light, which can be installed close to the corners and painted to match the color of the wall, making it less obtrusive.

Long drops from second or third landings can often be the perfect place through which to hang a dramatic pendant. If you want to use this light source to shed light onto all of the landings, you will need to consider a design of fixture that casts light along its entire length and not just from a single fixed point at the end of the flex. Do not try to recess lights into the sloping underside of a staircase. There is usually insufficient recess depth, and the light fixture is likely to cause glare as you go up and come down the stairs.

Positioning the controls

Once you have selected the various types of light sources and their locations, you need to consider the locations of the controls carefully so you can knit the spaces together effectively. Deciding on the locations of the controls for the lighting on your landings and in your stairwells can be confusing, as there

Softly efficient
LED wall-recessed fixtures wash the stair treads with a soft light. These economic 1-watt fixtures provide great energy savings compared to the standard 20-watt/12-volt option.

are so many variations on how these types of spaces can be used. It is worth taking the time to work out how you are most likely to move through the space. There are two key things you need to ensure you are able to do. First, if you are at the base of the stairs ready to go upstairs, can you turn all the lighting off in the hallway area and turn on lights for the stairs and first floor landing? Secondly, once on a landing, can any person leaving a room easily reach a switch to turn on a light so they can see where they are going? Once you have sorted this out, it is easier to build a logical arrangement of switch plates while keeping the number of plates to a minimum. There is no right or wrong way to arrange the controls in this kind of space, and it is often very useful to get professional advice on this aspect of your lighting plan.

Using dimmers

If you propose to control the lighting in a staircase using manual dimmers, do give some thought as to the best position for the dimmer switches. It is likely that you will want to position the dimmer in the most convenient location for that area. If you are using a more sophisticated dimming control, such as a push-button dimmer or wireless system (see pages 42–45), you will be able to dim from any point.

Ensure that you keep the number of switches to a minimum, avoiding unnecessary clutter on the walls. Also, aim to position the wall plates 35 inches (90 cm) from floor level. This places them in line with door handles and out of eye line.

Being able to maintain your lighting is a key part of a good scheme. If you are never going to be able to reach a fixture to change a bulb, choose a different lighting solution. Make sure that wherever you place them, your lights are easily accessible for maintenance.

◄ **Calming measure**
Low-level stair washers
provide practical light,
while up/down lights hug
the curved back wall of
the landing, allowing the
architectural forms to
stand alone without
further decoration.
This creates a relaxed
ambience, pulling together
the variety of wooden,
metal and glass materials
used in the space.

▲ **Line of sight**
Low-level linear LED
lighting concealed in a
channel provides practical
lighting in keeping with
the minimalist design of
the stairwell.

Key tips

■ Position a light fixture only where it can be
maintained easily.

■ Consider the locations of control plates to
ensure the spaces are visually connected and
work effectively.

■ Recess lights into the fabric of the
building, such as in staircase walls, window
ledges, and so on, to increase your options in
small or restricted spaces.

■ If you use a pendant to light a staircase,
choose one that will provide light to all of
the landings.

Living rooms

Your living room should be the relaxing heart of your home and a place in which to welcome guests and make them feel at ease. The space should encourage conversation and promote easy social interaction. The lighting in this room is a vital tool for creating this atmosphere.

When planning the lighting scheme in your living room, consider the furniture layout. If the main seating area is in the center of the space, ensure you anchor each corner with a table lamp. This may mean you need to install electrical sockets in the floor so you can position the lamps where you need them but avoid the hazard of trailing wires.

A table behind a sofa is a useful place to locate a pair of lamps to light the seating area. This removes clutter from side tables and puts the lamps in a slightly higher position, which is more useful for reading. If you opt for gold-lined shades to provide extra warmth to the light, you will want to use a discreet floor-standing reading light (see pages 150–153).

For a seating area arranged around the walls, a pair of lamps, either floor standing or on accent tables at either end of the sofa,

▲ Centerpiece seating
The focal points in this living room, over the fireplace and over the coffee table, are strongly lit with ceiling-recessed spotlights that draw people to the center of the main seating space.

◄ Symmetrical harmony
A pair of table lamps provides useful reading light around the sofa and frames the mirror. These are flanked by wall lights that function as wall decoration and add a warm layer of light. The chandelier draws the eye to the central focal point and grounds the space.

will provide the light you need. If you are short on space, or want to create a clutter-free space, wall-mounted swing-arm lights set at a height of approximately 4¼ feet (130 cm) from the floor are a good way to supply reading light around a sofa. If you have a central coffee table or a dining or games table, consider using a floor-standing arc lamp to shed a large pool of light over it.

In a compact living room, you can inject a warm glow without lamps by fitting a standard-voltage rope light along shelving or an incandescent halogen light source on top of storage units. Always position this type of lighting with care to ensure you cannot see the bulbs from any angle—particularly when seated.

Lighting focal points
To draw the space together, it is a good idea to balance the lamp light in the room by highlighting a select few

focal points to pull the eye around the space. One option is to add extra layers, such as a pair of wall lights. Position them at a height of around 5¾ feet (175 cm) from floor level. Whether they are simple plaster rectangles or highly decorative pieces, they will frame the elevation and help to balance out the light in the room, encouraging you to use the whole space, not just the main seating area.

Use low-voltage spotlights to highlight focal points, such as a painting or a mirror over a fireplace. However, if the focal point is a flat-screen TV, do not be tempted to light it—TV screens look awful when lit. You can introduce other focal points to the space, for example, by uplighting the jambs of a traditional fireplace or positioning low-voltage floor-standing uplights behind pot plants. The latter is a good way of eradicating

"dead" corners. Consider lighting decorative curtains, particularly if you always close them at night.

Key tips

- Consider the furniture layout and position lamps accordingly.
- Use a small number of large lamps rather than many small lamps.
- If you cannot recess lighting in the ceiling, introduce low-voltage lights by using plug-in uplights to highlight focal points or works of art.
- Always fit dimmers to each lighting circuit in a living room.
- If you need a reading light, invest in a minimalist floor-standing reading light designed for the task.

▼ ▶ Two-tone
Simple lighting highlights the artwork, while the lamps provide a welcome decorative addition at dusk (below left). Floor-recessed electrical sockets are hidden under the sofa to prevent trailing wires.

The space is transformed at night (below right) by dimming the lighting and adding layers via the lighting in the adjacent dining room and the yard. The latter serves to extend the sense of space.

▶ **Understanding the layers**

Directional spotlights are sparingly used to light the artwork and central coffee table. Table lamps provide essential ambience.

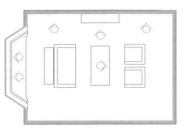

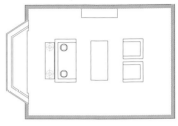

Layers 1 & 2 Ceiling-recessed spotlights

Layer 3 Table lamps and floor sockets

Key

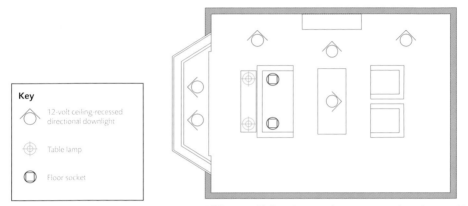

12-volt ceiling-recessed directional downlight	
Table lamp	
Floor socket	

All layers All lighting layers combine to create a calm and cozy ambience

Kitchens

The kitchen is the room in which people tend to spend the most time. Task lighting is the most important element to get right. Most kitchens are overlit without actually providing the best working light. Moreover, since for most of us the kitchen is as much a living space as a practical space, multiple layers of lighting come in handy.

Ideally, in the kitchen you want to work in shadow-free light. For countertops against a wall or under wall-mounted cabinets, consider positioning directional spotlights in line with the edge of the countertop. Angle the light to bounce off the wall or cabinets and back toward you. This means that the light will fall in front of you without casting a shadow, enabling you to see what you are doing.

In a narrow galley-style kitchen, this type of directional lighting will also help to open out the space.

If you have tall cabinets or wall units with at least 12 inches (30 cm) of space above, use a linear light source, such as a warm white fluorescent, a linear low-voltage or a linear LED to create a diffused light. You need at least 12 inches (30 cm) between the top of

▲ Neat definition
The working area of this kitchen is neatly highlighted with low-voltage recessed spots. These highlight the objects placed on the glass shelf and push light through to the countertop. Another layer of recessed directional spotlights in the ceiling adds a shadow-free working light. The elegant colored-glass pendants provide an "eye stop" between the working and relaxing areas of the kitchen.

◄ Restrained elegance
Flush recessed under-cabinet lights provide unobtrusive task lighting to the countertop. A gentle ambient light is created with the use of an LED linear source located on top of the kitchen cabinets. A pair of hanging pendants adds light to an island (unseen) and provides a focal point as well as practical light.

the cabinets and the ceiling to allow the light to bounce back off the ceiling. If the space is narrower, the light is squashed and adds no useful working light.

Lighting working areas
Make the most of wall-mounted kitchen cabinets by inserting a light source underneath them to provide direct task lighting to the countertops. It is always cleaner and more discreet to recess the light source—LEDs work particularly well in this situation, as they won't heat up the contents of the cabinets above. If you need to mount fixtures on the surface, try to disguise these with a down-stand. If you have the space, or do not have wall-mounted cabinets, an incandescent halogen wall light will add indirect light and will create a more relaxing mood for eating than would lots of overhead spotlights.

A kitchen island needs to be well lit if it is the main area for food preparation. If your ceiling is above 7¾ feet (2.4 m) you can consider using hanging pendants for this purpose. Standard-voltage versions are preferable, as they add to the atmosphere and provide a focal point. A neat LED pendant might look cute, but it will not provide you with sufficient practical light.

Key tips

■ Use directional fixtures set in line with the base cabinets for shadow-free working light.

■ Guard against overlighting the space. You need less light than you think. Every fixture should have a task; if a light does not have a task, you don't need it.

■ Well-positioned under-cabinet lights provide task light and useful additional lighting in the working areas of a kitchen in the early morning and late evening.

■ A decorative pendant or a series of pendants over an island or table add atmosphere and help to break up solid lines of kitchen cabinets.

■ Circuit the lights in your kitchen separately to allow you to choose which lights you need when.

Modern lines

Rectangular and square low-glare ceiling-recessed spotlights wash light down the front of the cabinets and highlight the central island, adding a contemporary feel to this kitchen. Hidden low-voltage lighting is used in a niche (at left) to highlight flowers and expand the sense of space. Additional lighting over the stove is provided by integral lighting within the hood. If possible, it is always worthwhile to integrate this lighting into the main lighting control in the room for ease of use.

info **Light the floor**

Create drama by adding light into the toe kick of the kitchen cabinets to wash across the floor. You can choose either round or square versions. These provide a useful night-light, as well as a light that you can leave on when you have finished cooking. You will need to have a toe kick of at least 4 inches (10 cm) in depth.

▶ **Unexpected twist**
Highlighting the functional aspects of a kitchen, a linear LED light source provides intermediate light and highlights the open storage for china and glass. Floor-recessed uplights add definition to the space, while a classic wall-fitted task light adds working light and a warm ambience to make the space feel welcoming.

Dining rooms

In order to create a space you really want to use every day, as well as one in which to entertain and impress your guests on special occasions, you need to consider what type of lighting will work both during the daytime and evening. If you get it right, the result can be like adding an extra room to your home.

info

A room lit only by standard-voltage light sources will often feel too "flat." To remedy this, use a low-voltage plug-in floor-standing uplight to fill dead corners, or place a tabletop spotlight on a sideboard to illuminate a sculpture or other work of art. Experiment with different types of plug-in lights to create a more dynamic and interesting room.

The light over the table is the most crucial element to get right in a dining space. A strong focal point over the table inclines people to gather around it. If your ceiling is high enough—over 7¾ feet (2.4 m)—a decorative pendant is a great way to add visual interest. A standard-voltage light source will always give the most flattering light. The conventional solution that usually works well is a single pendant fixture over the center of the table, but if your table is long enough, opt for a pair or even a multistranded pendant to add drama. If you have a

▲ Enveloping warmth
The soft ambience in this dining room is created by picture lights. These provide an enveloping, warm atmosphere for the seated diners. Low-voltage spotlights highlight the table, while the lighting on the deck beyond provides interest and extends the sense of space.

◄ Plug-in ambience
In this very plain space, the light creates all the visual interest needed. Floor-recessed wide-beam LED uplights provide an architectural vista along one wall. Floor-based plug-in square uplights pick out the texture of the wide shutters and draw the eye toward the high ceiling. A minimalist rectangular low-glare double spotlight discreetly highlights the table.

very high ceiling, consider the drop of the pendant carefully. It is much better to hang a fixture lower than you think you should. You should still be able to see the person sitting opposite you, but the lower the light fixture, the better the atmosphere around the table will be.

If possible, cross-light a pendant with ceiling-recessed spotlights. These add a sparkle to glass and china in the evening and can boost light levels during meals in the daytime. Circuit the fixtures separately so you can adjust the amount of light you need in different areas depending on the occasion. A more contemporary look can be achieved using low-voltage ceiling-recessed spots. Use these in a line along the center of the table or to cross-light around table. Remember, it is the table you want to light, rather than the tops of the diners' heads.

Peripheral light

It is also important to position peripheral light appropriately. Either wall lights or picture lights are good choices, making for a cozy atmosphere in the evening and creating a space-widening impression during the day. Use low-voltage spotlights to enhance works of art or mirrors and wash light down drapes. If you have interesting windows and do not intend to close your drapes or blinds, recess miniature LED or low-voltage uplights into window sills or even the floor to uplight the architectural detail of a window or fireplace.

Key tips

■ If the ceiling is high enough, opt for a standard-voltage pendant as the focal point over your table.

■ Picture lights and wall lights work well in a dining room, as they provide a soft, ambient light at an intermediate level.
■ Light the curtains. There is nothing worse than a blank patch of fabric at night.
■ A pair of thin candlestick lamps, placed on a sideboard or console table, will provide soft background light during the meal.
■ The most flattering light always comes from candlelight, so have plenty of candles on the table to make everyone look and feel good.

Understanding the layers

These diagrams show how the layered lighting in the dining room pictured opposite was achieved.

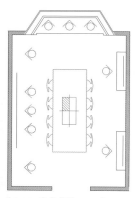

Layers 1 & 2 Recessed directional downlights and pendant lights

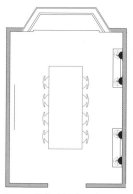

Layers 3 & 4 Wall sockets and table lamps

Key

⬠	12-volt ceiling-recessed directional downlight
▱	240-volt decorative pendant light
⊕	Table lamp
▲	Wall socket

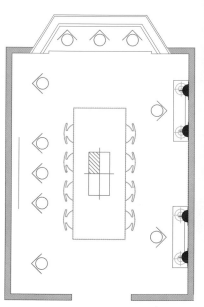

▲ All layers combined

A distinctive decorative pendant highlights the focal point — the table. Ceiling-recessed lights draw the eye to the wall-hung artwork, and table lamps give a soft, ambient light when the diners are seated.

Sparkling centerpiece
A spectacular contemporary rectangular chandelier provides a central focal point over this dining table. The ceiling-recessed directional spotlights in the bay window ensure that space is not lost at night and also wash the walls with light, expanding the sense of space and highlighting the pictures on the walls.

Open-plan living

The key to successful lighting in an open-plan living area is to circuit the lighting to provide the control you need to "partition" the space. Use the light to divide the area, allowing you to create focus in one part of the room before you then move into the next.

Most open-plan living areas include kitchen, seating and dining areas. You need practical lighting in a kitchen, relaxing lighting in a living room and an intimate light in a dining room. When planning your lighting circuits, take into account the lighting elements that might be linked together—for example, a circuit of table lamps that takes in both the living and dining areas. Whenever one area is in use, you need to feel that the adjacent area is still there, and a low-level ambient light is an ideal way to maintain the feeling of spaciousness of an open-plan space without loss of atmosphere.

▲ ▼ Clever cohesion
A one-room control system is used to "unlock" the individual elements of this open-plan space, linking the living room with the kitchen. Lighting in both rooms is designed to draw the eye between the two spaces. Pockets of light created by lit niches give a living-room style of light to the kitchen, and the up/down lights used in both spaces enhance the visual link between them.

▲ Layered living
The combined layers of light throughout the space pull this open-plan room together to create a welcoming ambience. The high ceiling is both highlighted and warmed using low-voltage linear lighting set discreetly in an up-stand so that it does not reflect in the windows at the sides.

Tip

If an island is used to separate kitchen and living areas, a good way to provide a visual divider is to hang some skinny pendants over it. These will provide practical light for food preparation and a subtle delineation of the areas.

Do not skimp on the number of lighting circuits you install. This does not mean that the only way to light this type of space successfully is to flood it with lots of light, but rather that the lighting that you do use should be separately controlled. This is what will give you the flexibility to highlight one area while the others take more of a backseat.

At a minimum, allow at least two circuits for each area, although three will give you more flexibility. In the kitchen area allow for under-cabinet lights, practical overhead lights and something special over the island. In the living area, table and floor lamps are still key, as are recessed low-voltage directional spotlights and light within shelving or niches. The dining area requires focus over the table as well as table lamps or wall lights and peripheral spotlights. The table-lamp circuit will pull the areas together and will probably become one of the most used circuits, especially if combined with under-cabinet lights in the kitchen.

Don't forget to work with the focal points in each area. These are especially important, as you need to consider how each area looks from another. The pendants over an island in the kitchen, the lit painting facing the main seating area and the light over a dining table will be the first things that people notice when they enter the space.

Positioning the controls

Once you have decided which lighting elements you want in each area, consider how you want to control the lighting and where you want to position the controls. It is worthwhile to use a small control system (see pages 42–45) that will allow you to mix the lighting circuits, from day into afternoon, evening and late-evening scenes that can be instantly accessed at the touch of a button.

If you have manual dimmers, careful consideration of their location is important. You don't want to sit down at the dining table and then have to walk back to the kitchen to alter the lighting levels. If you choose to use manual controls, position them 3 feet (90 cm) from floor level—in line with door hardware. This takes them out of people's eye line. The less clutter in the space, the more seamless it will feel.

Key tips

■ Circuit the lighting separately to allow you to use the space flexibly.
■ In really large spaces, consider using a small one-room control system to make setting scenes effortless.
■ Consider the focal points in each area and circuit them accordingly.
■ Lamp light will be the most important "connecting" theme throughout the space, so don't skimp on the electrical sockets.
■ Make sure you locate the controls where you need them most.

Understanding the layers
This layered approach to lighting enables this multifunctional space to be used to its best advantage.

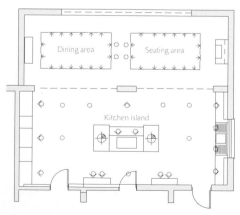

Layers 1 & 2 Ceiling-recessed lights and pendants combine with lights set within the skylights.

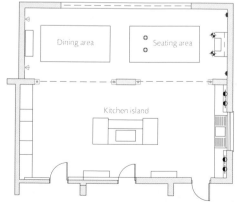

Layers 3 & 4 Recessed under-cabinet LED lights, wall-mounted up/down lights, floor-recessed uplights, floor sockets for lamps, and decorative wall lights.

▲ **Unified elegance**
The lighting in this open-plan living area demonstrates how a layered approach with separate circuiting and a one-room control system creates a practical yet elegant multifunctional space.

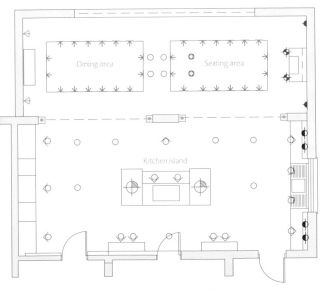

Dining area

Seating area

Kitchen island

All layers All lighting combined for a fully layered effect.

Key	
⊘	12-volt ceiling-recessed directional downlight
○	12-volt ceiling-recessed fixed downlight
⤲	12-volt semi-recessed ceiling-mounted up/down light
◕	Recessed under-cabinet LED light
◉	12-volt wall-mounted up/down light
⊕	12-volt floor-recessed uplight
⊕	Decorative pendant
◁	Decorative wall light
◀	Wall electrical socket
⊙	Floor electrical socket

Children's rooms

Clean, fresh, practical light is essential in a playroom. Simple layers of light should provide brightness for serious play and a dimmed, softer light for calmer activities, such as story time. The position of any visible fixtures is also important, as every element in the lighting scheme should be out of reach of young children.

Lighting in a playroom needs to be bright enough to be able to see everything clearly, including toys and activities on the floor, and it has to be welcoming. This is one of the few rooms in the house where you can never have too much light—as long as it is dimmable. Consider installing one separate circuit of low-voltage downlights for in-fill light directly over the floor area to ensure sufficient shadow-free light in the center of the space.

If you are unable to recess lights into the ceiling, consider placing incandescent halogen, linear fluorescent or linear LED light sources on top of any storage units to bounce shadow-free light off the ceiling. Alternatively, choose wall lights with a linear incandescent halogen light source.

Task lighting for children

Older children need a well-lit desk space for reading, drawing and homework. It is always better to keep the surfaces clutter-free by adding lighting under an overhead shelf —for example, with LED under-cabinet lights or a wall-mounted LED flexi-light or lamp to provide task light. LED is a cool source of light and, therefore, a safe choice for areas used by children. Keep the control for this

◄ **Pretty in pink**
Halogen energy-saving lamps to light the desk space and bedside table are a practical solution for a children's room. The choice of pink gingham shades adds a pretty glow to the room.

▲ **Secret space**
Concealed by a down-stand, a linear low-voltage light fitted into the understair area transforms this storage space into an attractive activity area for a child. Niche lighting in the colored cubes adds to the effect.

light source near the desk so the light levels can easily be adjusted by the person who is working there.

Frontlight or backlight to bookshelves will create a cozy atmosphere for reading. Use wall-mounted lights, set at approximately 4¼ feet (130 cm) from floor level, to provide reading light without cluttering the floor with lamps and wires.

Always remember that, while bright colors can look good in a playroom, colored light is not very practical. It is best to inject character and fun in the space by hanging simple strings of colored lights on walls or installing colored wall lights.

Key tips
■ Plan ahead and include electrical sockets for lamps for use as your child grows.
■ Include at least one separate circuit of light-boosting in-fill.
■ If you install built-in storage, try to incorporate some hidden light within the units.
■ Backlit or frontlit shelves and wall-mounted reading lights will create cozy reading corners.
■ Task light for a desk should be locally controlled so it is easy to adjust.

Home offices

Good working light is essential for a productive home office, study or den. Always begin with the direct task light to the key work area and plan outward from there. Consider introducing a layer of indirect glare-free light to create the best environment for work with a computer.

Consider the location of your desk before deciding on the type of task light. If the desk is freestanding, plan to install floor electrical sockets to avoid an unsightly tangle of cables. Specific task lights, such as the classic Anglepoise or a more modern LED equivalent, make better work lights than do table lamps, which do not provide sufficient light. Additional generalized overhead lighting must be positioned carefully so as not to cause shadows. Opt for wide-beam lamps, such as 40-degree beam widths, and use a honeycomb louver to avoid glare (see page 67).

Lights can also be installed under overhead shelves directly above a desk, although always take care to consider the location of a computer screen to avoid glare and reflections. Indirect shadow-free light, the best source if you work a lot on a computer, is best achieved with wall-mounted uplights (which are best set approximately 6½ feet/ 2 m from floor level if your ceiling is 7¾ feet/2.4 m or higher). A similar effect

◀ **Coolly minimalist**
This perfectly poised task light sheds glare-free light onto the desk. Colored uplights between the planters on the balcony beyond create a serene extended working space.

▶ **Studied restraint**
Linear fluorescent tubes, softened by frosted glass under the shelves, light the storage area. Two tall table lamps provide task light, without causing unwanted glare on the computer screens.

can be achieved by installing incandescent halogen, LED or fluorescent lamps on top of any built-in furniture or freestanding storage. Bookshelves or open storage units lit by a standard-voltage light source will inject warmth, making the space more attractive to work in.

If you have a large study or den with a sofa where you read, position a pair of table lamps with large shades at each end of the sofa.

Alternatively, choose a reading light, such as a slim floor-standing task light, to provide bright light wherever needed.

If your study is a desk or table in the corner of the kitchen, maximize the space by using a wall-mounted task light. A desk area under the stairs demands two sources of light. You will need one practical light source, such as a baffled linear fluorescent incandescent tube set under the slope of the stairs, which will

give you good working light. You will also want a more attractive light, such as a fabulous desk lamp that can be left on when the rest of the room is in "play" mode. Circuit the desk light with the rest of the room, but control the working light locally so it can be switched off when not in use.

Key tips
■ Invest in the best specific task light you can afford.
■ Indirect shadow-free light is the best option if you work primarily on a computer.
■ Light any fixed open storage units, either from within or from the ceiling, to soften hard lines and to add texture and depth to a space.
■ Consider placing reading lights near the chair or sofa where you read.

◀ **Pockets of light**
A wall-mounted classic task light creates a clearly defined task light to the working area of a kitchen.

tip Dual use

In many homes, the demands on space mean that desk space is often fitted into a room that has another primary function. Imaginative lighting solutions are needed to make sure both uses are catered for. Here, layers of light that permit multiple tasks enable a dressing room to double as a study space.

▶ **Study space**
Linear shelf lights highlight the books in this desk area and provide an appealing clutter-free task light at night.

1 Linear lighting concealed on top of the closets provides shadow-free working light to the desk as well as practical dressing light.

Concealed low-voltage lighting provides reflected light to the room

2 A ceiling-recessed spotlight provides specific working light over the desk. Side lighting is introduced with a standard-voltage linear light source under the shelves in the alcoves to the left and right of the desk.

Ceiling-recessed spotlight provides work light to the desk

3 An intimate nighttime lighting scheme is created by dimming the general lighting and leaving the shelf lighting on.

Linear standard-voltage shelf lighting provides a low-key night-light

Wine cellars

The place in which prized bottles of wine are stored not only needs to be lit to show off its contents, but also to serve the practical purpose of enabling you to read the labels. Whether it is a separate room where atmosphere is key, or a glass box tucked into spare space, the lighting should create a sense of drama.

In order to light a wine cellar successfully, you need to understand the layout of the space and how the wine is racked. Even the smallest wine cellar should have focal points and layers of light. Sharp contrasts between light and shadow will create the necessary impact.

The temperature of the lighting is a key element to consider. Most good-quality wine cellars are temperature-controlled, and it is advisable to employ cool sources of light, such as LEDs. Always opt for a long-life light source, but the lighting still needs to be accessible for maintenance. LEDs, standard-voltage linear rope lights or fiber optics are a good choice if you plan to backlight wine racks.

If the wine cellar is underground, the lighting on the steps needs to be practical enough to enable you to easily access the space safely and enticing enough to draw you in. Consider fixtures that wash the stairs with light, or design the steps with a nosing so you can incorporate a linear light source.

Recess small low-voltage or LED uplights to highlight divisions between racks. If your wine storage area is small or has a glass wall separating it from other living areas, a good solution is to use Plexiglas racks lit with linear LEDs, which will make the space glow from within. In a separate wine cellar, if the racking allows, consider positioning linear light sources on top of the racks to provide uplighting. This is especially effective in a barrel-vaulted ceiling. Create some individual

Show time
The eye is easily drawn into this wine cellar. Ceiling-recessed spots sharply highlight the wooden wine boxes and make it easy to find the right bottle in a moment. The lighting in the foreground is kept soft using a pair of lamps, further enhancing the visual pull.

Aged finesse
Cleverly positioned low-voltage spotlights highlight the bottles in their racks and enhance the traditional structural elements of this wine cellar.

niches to add depth to the space and contrast to the regularity of stored wine bottles.

If the wine cellar is designed as a space in which to spend time—for example, to host wine tastings—then the table must be well lit. A decorative pendant will create atmosphere, and a wrought-iron design is a good choice for a brick-lined vault. Wall lights set at the right height will add to the atmosphere.

Consider the location of manual controls so that the lighting can be turned on from any of the rooms that have a view of the wine cellar.

Key tips

■ If it is designed to be seen by visitors, the wine cellar should have dramatic, almost theatrical lighting.

■ Sharp contrasts between light and shadow work well against brick and glass.

■ Always opt for cool light sources to ensure that excess heat does not spoil the wine.

■ Control of the layers of light is important, particularly if the wine storage can be seen from other rooms.

■ One lighting layer should provide light for reading wine labels. This should be dimmable and separately circuited.

info Laundry rooms

Laundry rooms, particularly those without natural light, need to be well lit to ensure good color recognition and provide sufficient practical light for ironing and other domestic tasks.

It is always a good idea to consider energy consumption, but the laundry room is possibly the easiest room in which to put these principles into practice. You will find a good-quality daylight white or warm white fluorescent tube provides the most economic and practical light for the laundry room. As a functional space, the laundry room requires good overall shadow-free light, which you can achieve by employing wall-mounted up/down lights. Where space is restricted and the walls are taken up with storage, consider installing daylight white fluorescent tubes on top of the storage units. This form of lighting facilitates color recognition when sorting laundry.

Energy-efficient task lights in the form of under-cabinet lights provide good practical light to any work surface, especially if there is little space for wall-mounted lights. If these have to be surface-mounted fixtures under wall-mounted cabinets, add a baffle or down-stand so they are less obvious and cast a glare-free working light.

If you plan to hang laundry on a drying rack suspended from the ceiling, ensure that you do not position any light source directly above these areas; the light will be blocked when you hang out your laundry and there could be a fire risk. Use spotlights to wash light down built-in storage for reflected light.

If you have enough room, add character and some softness by introducing some attractive utility-style wall lights around the main working area or sink. Although it is always useful to dim lighting, it is often more practical to simply switch the lights on and off in a laundry room.

Media rooms

A room used primarily for watching movies and television needs to ooze drama when most of the lights are off. However, the lighting effects must be subtle enough not to compete with the action on the screen, so subtle layering and control is key.

Overhead lighting is not a necessity for a media room, unless it has to double up as a playroom or living room at other times. So, for the purpose-built media room, work with indirect sources of light. Keep all lighting away from the main screen. Coffered ceilings are a good solution (see pages 108–113). These add both the illusion of height and, if you choose a warm source of linear light such as standard-voltage rope light, will create a subtle background glow.

If you can't coffer the ceiling, consider using fiber optics to create a starry sky effect.

▲ Laid back
An effortless and restful background light is created in this den by using a standard-voltage linear light source tucked above and below the media storage unit. The line of light continues under the fireplace to lengthen the space.

▶ Movie magic
A warm 230-volt linear light source backlights the recessed shelves for perfect ambient light for watching movies.

This solution works best if you attempt to replicate a part of the solar system using a variety of large and small fibers to represent different stars and planets.

Linear lighting

For an art-deco style that lends a glamorous, retro feel to the room, hide linear light sources behind offset "fin-style" walls. This provides an excellent background lighting for watching movies. If the floor is sloped or stepped, consider recessing low-voltage floor washers into the walls to enable people to see

Lighting options

Wall units around a screen can be fitted with different lighting options for each type of activity for which a multifunction room is designed. Low-level lighting around a screen is best for watching television or movies.

From play space to movie theater
1 Bright ceiling-recessed spotlights ensure this basement media room and den doubles up as a fun and practical play space during the day. A well-lit floor space is essential in a playroom. A second circuit of peripheral recessed spotlights lights the artwork to provide points of interest.
2 The use of a control system enables the mood of the room to be changed at the touch of a button. An early-evening feeling is created by dimming the overhead lighting and introducing the concealed lighting in the book niches.

where they are going and provide a soft, background light. Low-level linear lighting can be installed under the nosing of steps. You can also use linear lights to create a "floating" coffee or accent table.

If the media room doubles up for another use, consider how the room will look when the screen is not in use. A strong focal point is needed for when a drop-down screen is up. A large painting, for example, can be specifically lit and separately circuited to allow the lighting to be turned off when the screen is down. Similarly, if you have a fixed wall-mounted flat-screen TV, create a visual diversion for when it is not in use by lighting other focal points.

It is essential to plan your lighting circuits. If you are going to the trouble of creating a special space for watching movies, a control system is a must (see pages 42–45). Install

3 The layers of light are further reduced to create a pre-movie mood. The in-fill light in the center of the room is taken out of the lighting scene, leaving only the dimmed peripheral spotlights.

4 As the screen is dropped down, the lighting is further reduced for an improved screen contrast. The lighting in the bookcase and to the artwork provides a subtle background light that does not detract from the images on the screen.

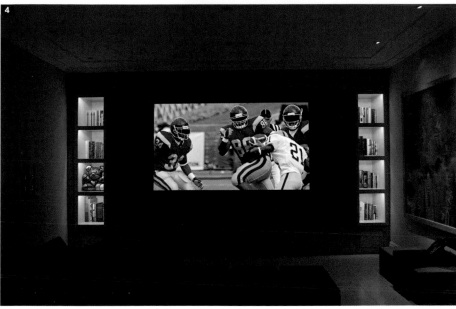

either a small one-room control system that will allow you to change the mood at the touch of a button or a more complex system with hand-held controls.

Key tips

■ Avoid all overhead lighting (unless being used for a special effect), and work with indirect light sources on all layers.

■ Keep direct light away from the screen.

■ Add special effects by employing fiber optics and introducing colored light sources for drama.

■ Consider how you want to control the lighting in the space right from the start. Take advice from a lighting designer and an audiovisual specialist to ensure you get exactly what you want.

Half baths

Often the smallest room in the house, half baths are often overlooked. As you are likely to use this space frequently, create ultra-flattering light. It will be a place your guests will remember.

The first place to start with is the lighting around the vanity, particularly to the mirror. If possible, create good lighting from above by using well-positioned recessed low-voltage spots. Set a single fixture, or a pair of fixtures about 24–32 inches (60–80 cm) apart, in line with the edge of the vanity. The light will bounce off the mirror and back to the face. Soften facial lines and introduce better skin tones by using wall-mounted lights on either side of the mirror approximately 60 inches (152 cm) from floor level.

Backlit solutions

In a more compact space and for an understated approach, backlight the mirror by creating a recess behind it. Stop the mirror short of the edge of the recess by at least 1¼ inches (3 cm), and fix the mirror so it appears to float in line with the edge of the recess. Position a linear light source that emits a soft, diffused light behind the mirror, so the mirror appears to float.

Strips of fluorescent light built into mirrored cabinets are often the least flattering option, as they tend to cause a flat, gray light. The same applies to built-in lights over mirrors, which will light the mirror and not your face.

Use the vanity to add light to the space. A suitable linear light source under the countertop will give a soft glow to the floor, but always prevent reflections in the floor. A shiny floor of any type will reflect back

▲ Strict elevation
Good lighting to the face is important to create an inviting feel in this small but important space. Here, a pair of well-proportioned wall lights not only gives excellent face lighting but creates a strong symmetrical elevation. This is softened by the concealed LED linear light set under the vanity, creating a floating effect.

▶ Paneled highlight
Wall-mounted bathroom lights, set just above eye level, provide good lighting either side of the face and reflect light off the sloping ceiling. This expands the sense of space and provides a soft, diffused light for a cozy feel.

◄ **Perfectly formed**
Recessed under-cabinet lights allow objects placed on the vanity to take center stage and add depth and visual texture to an otherwise dead space. The low-voltage light source also adds sparkle to the polished-chrome faucet. The countertop bowl is highlighted by a ceiling-recessed spotlight set directly above.

the light from even very small bulbs, which counteracts any illusion of floating. If the half bath has a disproportionately high ceiling compared to the floor space, a hanging pendant will create the effect of a lower ceiling and add a point of focus. In small half baths, maximize the sense of space by introducing lit niches, particularly behind the toilet.

Key tips

■ Concentrate on getting the best lighting to the face. A flattering light to the face is far more important than a practical light to the face in a half bath.

■ Consider not just wall lights either side of a mirror but ceiling pendant lights for an added touch of glamour.

■ Think about the view from the toilet and the wall behind the toilet. Use lights in niches to create visual focus.

■ Automatic control of lighting, at a pre-dimmed level, makes even the smallest room more user-friendly.

Bedrooms

The lighting in a bedroom should encourage calm and tranquility. The lighting should be gentle and glare-free yet allow for practical activity when required. A separate dressing room needs to be well lit, with particular attention paid to the lighting of mirrors.

You do not need a huge amount of light in a bedroom, and the main overhead lighting should be indirect. Use low-voltage lighting to wash walls and window treatments. This will highlight focal points and ensure that you don't get large swathes of blank fabric when the curtains are drawn at night. The overhead lighting circuit must be dimmable. One circuit should be dedicated to indirect light, while any infill light to the center of the room should be separately circuited so it can be turned off when not needed. If you have freestanding pieces of furniture that do not reach the ceiling, consider using a linear light source on top for an indirect light.

Bedside lights

Bedside lamps should be large, particularly if they are the only lamps in the room. Not only will large lamps give you a better reading

▲ Mellow minimalism

Architectural incandescent wall lights exude a soft indirect light in this bedroom. A linear warm white fluorescent light source, used behind the headboard wall, adds to the restful feel of this bedroom. Locally controlled wall-mounted bedside LED lights provide cool-to-the-touch reading light for each occupant.

◀ Complete picture

A pair of tall table lamps provides a traditional style of reading light at the bedside and serves to frame the headboard. Unobtrusive ceiling-recessed directional spotlights wash light down the walls, opening up the space and highlighting the drapes in the bay window, ensuring that this area is not "lost" at night.

light, but, as table lamps are the most used source of light in the room, they will add more ambient light to the space.

Some people prefer more direct light sources for reading. There are several options. A pair of ceiling-recessed spotlights can provide additional reading light. However, these must be positioned with great care, and the exact locations should take into account both the size and height of the bed and the height of the person sleeping in the bed. Otherwise the lighting may end up creating more shadow than useful light.

The alternative is to use an additional fixed light source close to the bed, such as a flexible bedside reading light (see page 126). An LED source is the best choice as it is cool to the touch (important when close to bare flesh). This type of light is best if locally controlled and is designed to cast a narrow beam to read by without disturbing your neighbor. If a more traditional look is desired, a swing-arm wall light (see page 126) is another option.

Ceiling-hung bedside lights can add a touch of glamour or a retro feel, depending on the style chosen. These are generally not the best sources of light to read by, but they make a stylish statement and keep the bedside clutter-free. The control of bedside light is an important consideration from the outset, particularly if separate controls for each side of the bed are required. One solution is to install the switches for the bedside lamps near the door and allow the reading lights to be locally controlled by their users.

Lighting at low levels will enhance a relaxed atmosphere and provide a night-light, if wanted. Consider recessing LED or low-voltage floor washers into the walls or into the toe kick of a built-in closet. Linear LED light sources are useful, as their tiny form can be incorporated easily into the shadowy gaps of closets. When considering the position of low-level lights, be sure to site them so you will not look directly into them when lying in bed. Ensure they are installed in a location in which the light helps you to find your way to the bathroom at night.

If you have a high ceiling, a decorative pendant fixture can provide a glamorous focal point. A pitched ceiling should be uplit to highlight the architecture and to provide a boost of general light. Always circuit these elements separately.

info Dressing rooms

Dressing rooms should always be well lit to enable you to see the colors of the clothes you are choosing. Well-baffled ceiling-recessed directional low-voltage spots can be positioned to wash down closet doors. This will open out the space and light the contents of the closet when the doors are open.

Another option to ensure that you can see the contents of your closets is to install lighting within. Fitting a door-operated switch which triggers the light on and off as you open and close the closet door is a good way to control this type of lighting. A daylight fluorescent tube will allow you to see color differences and, as a cool source of light, will not damage clothes.

Always consider the location of the mirror in the dressing space. If you have room, a pair of wall lights either side of a long mirror is a flattering way to light the body. A long mirror can also be backlit in the same way as described for a backlit mirror in the half bath. This approach will result in a soft ambient light when combined with a ceiling-recessed directional spotlight.

Chic simplicity
This simple dressing room is bathed in a practical light from ceiling-recessed lighting. The rectangular shape of the light fixtures works with the contemporary style of the space.

Don't forget to consider lighting for the dressing table. If the table is large enough, a pair of lamps will work well when combined with well-positioned overhead lighting. And even the smallest makeup space wedged into a built-in closet can be well lit.

Key tips

■ Use larger lamps than you think you need on bedside tables.

■ Ensure you have sufficient light for practical tasks.

■ Consider installing a night-light or two to guide you to the bathroom.

■ Consider the circuit arrangement to ensure that bedside lamps can be controlled separately if needed.

■ Put lighting in your closet. This is essential if you have dark wood interiors.

Easy on the eye

The use of either manual dimmers or a control system in a bedroom is a really useful tool to create a soft, relaxing atmosphere that will take you from practical dressing mode through the day and on to late-night reading.

1 Practical reflected light is created with miniature ceiling-recessed directional spotlights. These also pick out the detail of the closet door handles.

2 Wall-mounted swing-arm bedside reading lights are a practical addition when space is tight, and they add a warm ambience.

3 The overhead lighting is dimmed, leaving the wall lights to provide the main source of light for a more relaxed feel. Control plates located at the bedside make it easy to change the lighting mood as required.

4 With the overhead lighting turned off, a late-night atmosphere is easy to achieve by dimming the wall lights.

Bathrooms

When lighting a bathroom, treat it as you would a living area. This will result in a space that combines both practicality and a sense of serenity. Manipulate the lighting to soften the hard, reflective surfaces of mirrors, glass, marble and tiles.

The position of the overhead lighting in a bathroom is as important as it is in any other area where practical, shadow-free light is required. As when lighting countertops in a kitchen, position ceiling-recessed directional light in line with the edge of the vanity. Use either a single fixture centered over a sink, or a pair to cross-light the face. Be careful how you light the mirror. (See pages 118–123 for advice on this topic.)

The shower can be lit effectively by positioning ceiling-recessed downlights at the back of the shower cubicle to wash light down the back wall. As the eye is always drawn to the brightest point, this is the most successful way to extend the feeling of space in a bathroom. Downlights will pick out color and texture in tile, stone or marble for an

Amber glow
A linear LED light source hidden under the vanities stops them from feeling too heavy. This is complemented by the discreet backlit niches in the foreground. Overhead recessed spots give a crisp light to the face.

▲ Luxury lines
Simple wall lights are positioned at the best height to deliver lighting to the face. Elegant downlit linear slot niches add a touch of glamour, extend the sense of space and provide a useful shelf in the shower.

▶ Simple glamour
Beautiful decorative wall lights frame the large mirror in this bathroom. Ceiling-recessed spots lift light levels over the sink, and a downlit niche in the shower draws the eye through the space.

indirect light. Always avoid centering a light overhead in a shower cubicle. Not only is the light unflattering, but it has the effect of creating a "lit box" that detracts from the impression of space.

For added drama, recess cool-to-the touch LED uplights into the bath surround. If you have the luxury of a large freestanding bathtub, you can install lighting under it to create a floating effect. Soft lights can be inserted into walls at a low level, or a linear light source can be run under a vanity (but be aware of reflective floor surfaces) and under bathtubs for a gentle light to bathe by.

To create a dramatic focus in the shower, insert a slot-shaped niche to provide you with a built-in shelf for toiletries that can be downlit from within. This solution also prevents the shower from appearing as a black hole when the rest of the bathroom is lit with low-level lighting.

Colored lighting can be very effective in a bathroom. The most successful way to do this is either to create sharp contrast, for example, by inserting colored linear LED

▲ **Distinctive lines**
A backlit mirror softly diffuses light and provides excellent color rendition. Downlit niches are a useful night-light when dimmed.

◀▼ Discreetly obscured
This dressing table benefits from overhead lighting in the bathroom. When the shower is in use, a touch of a button obscures the dividing glass so that only a glow can be seen.

◀ Soft serenity
Cool-to-the-touch LED uplights highlight the unusual architecture in this attic bathroom. Overhead and low-level lighting in the shower is softly diffused through the frosted-glass screen.

(known as RGB, or red, green, blue) behind cantilevered Plexiglas or glass shelves, or to backlight panels with a soft diffused light. A blue hue will always be cooling, and pale green is the most relaxing. Yellow will uplift a space, and red will create a cozy atmosphere. This type of lighting can be controlled to scroll through primary colors as well as the tones and hues in between.

Key tips

■ Never use a direct overhead light in a shower.
■ Do everything possible to light the mirror well.
■ Always use at least two circuits in a bathroom, one for the practical light and one for a night-light or soft light to bathe by.
■ If installing recessed lights into tiled or mirrored slots or niches, use a fixture with a chrome, stainless steel or bronze bezel, which looks better than a white finish.
■ Create drama using fiber optics or LEDs to add punches of color to enhance the mood of the space.

info Safety

Electrical fixtures for bathrooms must be waterproof and tamper-resistant. When installing lighting in bathrooms, always ensure that you use a fixture that meets safety standards for this use. It is especially important to hire a qualified electrician for this kind of work. You will also benefit from the advice of a lighting designer, who will know which light sources to choose from the range to achieve the best results.

Understanding the layers
This combination of practical overhead lighting, specific mirror lighting and targeted niche and low-level lighting will satisfy a wide variety of requirements.

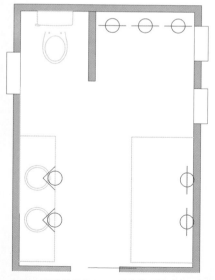

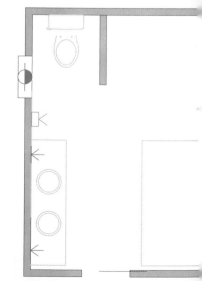

Layers 1 & 2 Ceiling-recessed directional downlights and ceiling-recessed fixed downlights.

Layers 3 & 4 Niche and low-level LED lighting. Low-voltage lighting to mirror.

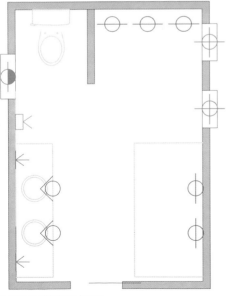

Layer 5 All lighting layers.

Layered texture
Multiple layers of light on several different circuits introduce texture and depth into this bathroom. Light washes down the back wall of the shower, drawing the eye through the space and highlighting the color and texture of the tiles. Dimmable mini LED "starlights" set into the mirror give an effective and flattering shadow-free light to the face.

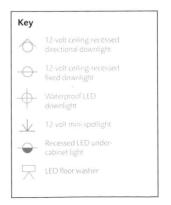

Key

⬡	12-volt ceiling-recessed directional downlight
⊖	12-volt ceiling-recessed fixed downlight
⊕	Waterproof LED downlight
↓	12-volt mini spotlight
◒	Recessed LED under-cabinet light
⊠	LED floor washer

Home gyms

A home gym should be filled with practical light, but nobody needs to work out under the glare of a spotlight. Simplicity is key. It is best to keep all light sources indirect and dimmable to create a space that is both energizing and restful.

As a general rule, you need less lighting than you think in a gym. The most important pitfall to avoid is that of peppering the ceiling with recessed downlights. There is nothing more irritating than to be working out on the floor and look up into the glare of a light source. Keep the lighting diffused. If the gym has plenty of mirrors, consider exploiting all angles of reflection to prevent glare. The color of any light source needs to be warm to avoid creating an unfriendly, cool feel in the space.

Energy and atmosphere

For practical lighting, concealed overlapping warm white fluorescent tubes in a coffered or dropped ceiling will give shadow-free reflected light. Alternatively, choose cold cathode or linear LED lights for a similar effect. If you want to create a mellower atmosphere for yoga or a more relaxed workout, install a parallel line of warm-colored standard-voltage rope light in the coffer. Be careful to ensure that these are on separate circuits for maximum flexibility.

◀ **Physically practical**
Wall-mounted uplights provide an indirect light in this gym for a glare-free workout zone. These can be dimmed to create a more relaxing atmosphere appropriate for floor-based exercises.

▲ **Cool color**
A cool, contemporary atmosphere is generated by the color-changing light hidden in this dropped ceiling. The blue light has an energetic feel. Unfussy rectangular recessed fixtures highlight the state-of-the-art equipment.

If recessed lighting in the ceiling is needed for general light, locate it around the edges so it washes the walls. Avoid using it over any area where floor work will take place. Wall-mounted uplighters can work well if you have sufficient ceiling height to reflect the light effectively. However, ensure the light fixtures will not impede any gym activity. Unless the space is large, other types of wall lights are best avoided for the same reason. All light fixtures should be strong enough to withstand the occasional knock.

Key tips
- Use indirect sources of light.
- Consider installing different light levels for different types of workouts.
- Locate any mirrors in such a way as to prevent glare.
- Keep fixtures clear of workout zones.
- Colored lighting can add style and ambience as well as fun.

Swimming pools

Indoor or outdoor, a swimming pool is primarily a place to exercise and relax, but it can be lit to double up as a fantastic party space. Practical lighting is key, but a carefully planned lighting scheme will allow you to transform the space into a dramatic backdrop for entertaining.

Start by considering how the pool itself should be lit, as this will be the foundation of your scheme, and work outward. It is essential that you have enough lighting in the pool for safety. The size and shape of the pool will dictate the amount of light that you need. Plan the location of the lighting wisely. Rather than placing lights at either end of the pool, which risks causing glare as you swim back and forth, skim light widthways across the pool to create a more restful result.

Types of light sources
Conventional low-voltage lighting is the most common light source used for pools, but a huge variety of fiber optics and LEDs, which are easier to maintain, are now available to create more dramatic effects. For example, a linear side-emitting fiber optic, which glows softly along its length, can be laid into the base of the pool to delineate swimming lanes.

Color concerns
You will also need to take the color of the pool tiles into consideration. Traditional blue tiles are easy to light, as are lighter tones, and mosaic tiles mixed with textured or metallic tiles. Darker colors require a lot more light. For example, dark green, dark gray and black pools look fine in bright sunshine, but they can end up resembling murky ponds at night if not lit with sufficient, well-positioned light.

Around the pool
Ensure there is sufficient light around the pool so those using the area can see well. Layer the light to achieve this effect instead of using a multitude of ceiling-recessed low-voltage spots. Simple effects have the greatest impact. For example, a number of low-voltage wall-mounted up/down lights set at an intermediate height between the floor and ceiling and using both narrow- and wide-beam bulbs create a dramatic play of light and shadow on the wall.

The same type of effect can be achieved by recessing LED uplights into the pool surround, so they skim light up a wall.

◄ Industrial touch
The lighting in this swimming pool emphasizes the natural textures and highlights the industrial architectural detail. The fiber-optic up/down lights in the large recess to the rear create a strong visual focal point.

▲ Tranquil space
A layered approach to lighting this pool area softens the hard architectural lines without losing the volume. The unusual use of a hanging pendant adds a note of tranquility.

Fiber-optic uplights, used in a similar way but with constantly rotating hues of color on a white or textured wall, create a stunning light show. A starry sky of fiber-optic pin spots above the pool, or over an adjacent spa, add an enchanting effect for swimming at night.

Practicalities

In the pool area, always use light fixtures designed for wet areas. You will also need to consider the finish of the fixture; stainless steel and anodized finishes have the longest life span in these conditions. The locations of light boxes, remote transformers and drivers all need to be considered in advance to ensure easy maintenance. Unless you are

▼ **Reflected glory**
Simple downlit slots around this swimming pool provide texture and depth to the space and create a strong architectural play of light on the water. Wall-mounted up/down lights behind the seating create an intermediate layer of lighting that balances the slots on the far wall.

using a control system, remember that standard switches need to be outside the pool area, but located in a position where you can see the lights you are controlling.

Key tips

■ Have enough light for safety but don't overlight the interior of the pool.

■ Consider the color of the interior of the pool. A black pool is not easy to light and may end up looking dark and uninviting.

■ Use light fixtures and finishes designed for wet areas, and do not install hot light fixtures where they may be underfoot.

■ Create drama by using lighting to highlight architectural details.

■ If the pool is outside or has windows overlooking a yard or deck, it is important to light the exterior space to encourage the eye to travel outward.

■ Maintenance is key. Do not put light fixtures where they cannot be reached.

◄ **Uplights**
Easy-to-maintain LED recessed uplights wash additional light up the immaculately plastered wall for a bright but glare-free reflected light.

▲ Enchanted effect
If lighting an outdoor pool, remember that a minimal approach often works best. Lighting set into the pool surround, supplemented by lighting in plants and on the deck, provides all the light needed for a subtle and enchanted effect.

▶ Strict lines
The planting visible through the structural slot is uplit to draw the eye outward to the yard beyond. Pool lights are positioned in such a way as to increase the apparent width of the pool.

Sunrooms

It is important to the think of a sunroom not simply as an extension to a house but as a part of the outdoor space. The lighting must connect it with the main dwelling but also to the yard beyond, creating a space that is inviting all year round. A successful sunroom is one in which you are inclined to spend time throughout the year.

In a sunroom, hard flooring and glass walls and ceilings limit the lighting options. Because of this, it is always easier if the lighting design is considered before the room is built, so that the design can be adapted, if necessary, to allow for good lighting.

Starlight effects

The expanse of glass is the first thing to consider. A series of small low-voltage capsule lights or LED "starlights" can be used at regular intervals around an up-stand around a pitched ceiling. This will give a good light to the space when it's used at full power, and when dimmed it will create a soft, gentle sparkle to detract from the blackness of overhead glass at night.

If any of the roof panes can be opened, then any lighting used must be suitably weatherproof. In this situation, fiber optics or LEDs are a better choice than regular low-voltage lights.

◀ **Glare-free sparkle**
Cowled mini LED spotlights add sparkle to this sunroom's roof while creating minimum glare below. This treatment prevents the glass from becoming mirrorlike at night.

▶ **Effective repetition**
A row of low-voltage up/down lights bring out the texture of the painted brickwork and create a space-enhancing sense of perspective.

▲ Lighting link
Cable lights are carefully positioned
in this sunroom to highlight the flower
arrangement on the table. The scheme is
complemented by the exterior lighting,
creating a harmonious whole.

Lighting the center

A decorative pendant is a great way to break up the space, providing a visual eye stop as well as supplying that all-important light over a dining table. Use incandescent bulbs in either simple plaster up/down lights or in more decorative wall lights to create an intermediate warm light. If your room is designed to be a sitting area rather than a dining area, plot out the best locations for electrical sockets in the floor for table and floor lamps. These are possibly the most important means of siting warm light at the heart of a room, making the space welcoming and usable.

info Porch lighting

Light a front porch as you would a living room. Build in layers of light to create a beautifully relaxed outside seating area and illuminate the external structure of the house.

Wall lanterns are a great way to create atmosphere on a front porch. Not only do these provide a welcoming light upon approaching the house, they also provide an intermediate ambient light to seating areas. Consider using specially sealed external standing lamps or organic-shaped floor lamps, just as you would table lamps in a living room (see also pages 168–169). These can boost the atmosphere of any scheme, but take care not to create too busy an arrangement so that the front of the house looks cluttered.

If the front porch has a sloping roof, use some surface-mounted low-voltage spotlights to skim light upward and highlight any architectural details. It is important to carefully position such fixtures so that the bulb cannot be seen.

Miniature LEDs can be used to uplight any supporting posts to the structure to highlight and add visual interest. Cool to the touch, these are an energy-efficient way to provide a low-key layer of light.

Outside living
An inviting outdoor seating area is created with the use of wall lights combined with uplighting and downlighting to highlight architectural details, providing depth and helping to draw the eye around the space.

◀ Warm welcome
The floor-based lamp in the corner of this sunroom is well placed to provide a barrier of warmth between the glass and the seating area. A cable system (unseen) uses low-voltage spotlights to illuminate the objects on the wall, highlighting and casting shadows.

▶ Shaping shadows
A cable system is a great way to introduce essential overhead light in a sunroom. In this example, narrow-beam lights highlight the wrought-iron feature on the wall, and a lantern-style wall light provides soft, ambient lighting.

Focus on the features

Strategically positioned surface-mounted low-voltage spotlights can be used to uplight the ceiling structure, but you need to consider where to locate any remote transformers.

Use floor-recessed uplights to pick out the structural elements, adding focus and depth to the room. If you have potted plants around the edges of the room, use low-voltage or LED spiked spots in the planters. These will highlight the plants and cast shadows through the leaves, adding texture and depth to the room. Finally, always consider how the yard, deck or any other exterior space will be lit so that you do not end up with sheets of black glass at night. Lighting a tree or a focal point outside immediately draws your eye outward and extends the sense of space.

Key tips

■ Remember to consider warm light for a cozy feel if you want to use your sunroom all year round.

■ If the sunroom has a pitched ceiling, get light up into that space to highlight the architectural detail and to prevent cold expanses of black glass at night.

■ If you use the sunroom as a living room, floor sockets are a must, enabling you to introduce warm low-level light to seating areas.

■ If you plan to dine in your sunroom, fit a decorative pendant over the table. This may need specific structural support, so specify this when planning the space.

■ Always consider the lighting beyond the sunroom. Even lighting a single tree in the yard can provide a key point of focus.

Outdoor spaces

Well-positioned, well-chosen light fixtures in the yard or on a deck will transform an exterior space, but they will also reinvent the adjacent interior spaces. A judiciously lit yard will extend the sense of space from the inside, giving you the feeling of having gained an "extra room" on the outside.

Yards and decks
A shimmering effect is created with waterproof low-voltage spotlights recessed in front of the water feature. The light skims up the brushed stainless steel fascia and through the water that gently trickles over it. Backlighting adds a silhouetted effect.

Approach lighting your backyard as you would your living room. Choose one or more focal points—for example, a tree, sculpture or some hard landscaping—that can be lit. Choose objects that will look good whatever the season. Next, consider what lighting might be needed closer to the house, such as lighting to outdoor eating areas or path lighting to draw the eye out from the house. Then look at providing in-fill and background lighting among plants to bring them into play when they are at their seasonal best. This approach will work with small as well as large outside spaces.

Fixtures for the backyard
Start by choosing fixtures that can be moved with the seasons for maximum flexibility, to help you match seasonal changes. Light fixtures that can be spiked into the earth are the most useful for flower beds and lawns. Always plan for at least 10 feet (3 m) of flex to allow you to move the fixture around as the seasons change and plants grow. Use spiked low-voltage or LED spotlights to highlight narrow plants or tree trunks, or use a spiked reflector-style fixture to wash light over wider areas of planting, uplight topiary or walls, or to create dramatic shadows. A ground-recessed uplighter is a more practical choice for uplighting larger objects or trees that do not rapidly change in width or height,

◀ **Interconnected levels**
Simple layered lighting enhances the architectural lines without crowding the space. This treatment allows the interior lighting to play a pivotal role in lighting the exterior. Submerged lighting in the pool adds further interest.

▼ **Natural textures**
Layers of lighting work subtly in this space to create an inviting outside living space without detracting from the focal point of the sculpture. Spiked low-voltage uplights skim light up the trees, providing a naturally textured backdrop to the seating area.

especially if the light is located in an area that needs to be mowed or has foot traffic.

Choosing colors

Choose the color of any fixtures used in the yard with care. The color needs to blend well with what it is lighting. A dark olive green works best in foliage, but black or copper are also good choices. However, in starker landscaping schemes, a fixture can work as a feature, as long as it is low glare and the bulb cannot be seen directly. A stainless steel fixture works well in such circumstances.

Lighting trees

Mature trees lend themselves to a simple but grand lighting gesture. A source of mercury vapor light can cast cool white light through broad canopies, creating a fairy-tale effect. In smaller yards try hanging lights in trees. This works particularly well when groups of different lengths of lights are hung randomly. Outside living spaces can be enhanced by using the increasing number of lighting options specially designed for external spaces, such as hard-wired freestanding lights that create a similar effect to lamps in a living room. The finish of this type of fixture

◀ Vertical highlights
Narrow-beam bulbs in wall-mounted low-voltage downlights make the most of the textured screen, highlighting the dark color of the clipped box hedging.

▶ Miniature miracles
Light cascades down the hard landscaping, directing the view to a water feature. The pool is not lit from within; it merely reflects overhead light.

▼ Sharp contrast
This hard architectural landscape is brought to life at night by the use of layers of light. The different levels of the space are highlighted, inviting your gaze to travel through the space to different zones. The plants are lit using flexible low-voltage spiked spots that can be adjusted to suit seasonal changes.

◀▲▶ Softly, softly
This dense style of planting is brought to life using low-voltage spiked spots and reflectors that wash light through the plants without obvious visual intrusion. A suitably rated concealed surface-mounted spotlight highlights the table (see detail at bottom left) to draw the eye to the seating area.

must be specifically designated as suitable for submerged or exterior use, such as an anodized finish or a 316 stainless steel. Quality is a prerequisite for durability.

Small spaces and color

Remember that, even in a tiny yard, a handful of spiked spots in planters or a few miniature ground-recessed LED uplights positioned between pots will transform a space. Colored light adds drama but works better in contemporary harder-edged spaces. The best results will always come from treating the backyard gently and painting it with light. The emphasis should be on the plants and other features, and not on the lights; the most successfully lit backyards contain the least evident light sources.

Key tips

■ Approach the lighting of any exterior space as you would the lighting of an interior space and plan to layer the light.

■ Seek out and light the focal points. Your yard will work much better if you have a lit object to draw the eye.

■ Consider how the lighting will look from all vantage points, including from all levels of the house.

■ A little light goes a long way outside, so you do not always need a lot to create an effect.

■ Safety and maintenance are important. Ensure you use suitably rated and finished fixtures, and have them installed by an expert.

Details

Light inserted into the most unexpected spaces will reap great rewards. If you need to pep up a space and cannot contemplate rethinking and rewiring a a room, there is still much you can do to highlight interesting details.

▲ **Economical impact**
An economical way to punch color into a space is to use linear fluorescent tubes within display storage. The light radiates through the colored glass to provide a visual feast.

One of the most straightforward things you can do is to light an interesting painting, curio or sculpture. You can use a portable plug-in solution (see pages 58–59). A tabletop spotlight or a floor-based plug-in directional uplight can create a focal point or introduce a soft silhouette. This is why, if possible, you should install as many sockets as you can, which gives you the flexibility to grow and develop a space.

Think ahead

If you plan to add storage to a living room or playroom but do not yet know what it might be, allow for wiring so you can insert lighting when your budget allows. Built-in furniture is always softened by the introduction of light. Consider the thickness of the shelves. If you want to add light later, you need a down-stand of at least 16 inches (40 cm) to ensure that any linear light source cannot be seen when you are sitting down. A 230-volt linear LED will highlight books and objects and provide useful background lighting. Combine linear lighting in storage units with pools of light from downlights or under-cabinet lights to highlight individual objects.

Avoid dead spaces

You can achieve impact by inserting light where it is least expected. For example, a half-landing or the area around the turn of a staircase, which is often a dead space, can be

▲ **Fabulous folds**
Lighting drapes prevents windows from turning into "dead areas" at night. It is also a great way to show off the textures and colors of beautiful fabrics and increase reflected light.

▶ **Seasonal adjustment**
Maximum impact is gained
from the natural texture of
the brickwork by the use of
inground low-voltage
uplights. Crucially, the
lighting maintains the
fireplace as a focal point
during the summer months.

◀ ▼ **Detailed delight**
A small injection of light into a limited
space creates instant impact.
Inground uplights provide a perfect
frame for the mirrored fireplace
feature (left). The plug-in square
uplighter (below) blends with the
color of the floor and is a subtle way
to reinforce the fireplace as the focal
point in the room.

revolutionized with simple treatment. A row of box niches, which can be used for display of collectibles or memorabilia, can be brought to life with the use of LED under-cabinet lights. These will also provide a night-light and lift what might otherwise be a lackluster space. They are a particularly good option if the area can be seen from several vantage points, such as from an entrance hall and upper landing.

Lighting details keeps you from treating a room like a square box. To create mood and soul you need to create depth and texture, which four bare walls will never do. Be brave and stretch the space to its maximum capability. Niches, trim, crown molding, window sills, wine racks, shelving and furniture all present opportunities to inject light and life into a room.

Key tips for lighting details

■ Think about special items or features you want to highlight and to which you'd like to draw attention.

■ If you are adding storage, take the opportunity to consider adding lighting into it.

■ Review dead spaces and think about how adding light may transform them.

■ Remember that even the most mundane areas, such as bottle storage, can be made into something special with the right type of lighting.

■ Even a square-boxlike room can be transformed by creating niches, slots and alcoves into which lighting can be set to provide a visual feast of depth and texture.

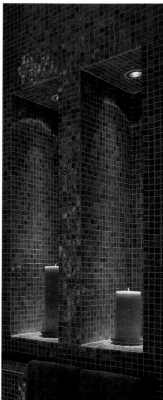

▲ **Sinuous silhouette**
The soft, curvaceous lines of the sculptural swan are backlit using a simple floor-based plug-in fitting. Clever positioning of the low-voltage tabletop spot on the floor places the swan into silhouette to create visual impact.

▶ **Instant iridescence**
Low-voltage downlights in these candlelit tiled niches create high-impact iridescent reflections.

Lighting objects of interest

A surface-mounted low-voltage or LED footlight can be used to light a statue or a vase on a shelf or within a bookcase. Take care to position the light source a suitable distance away from the object so as not to risk overheating the item.

Freestanding objects

These can be locally lit using a plug-in tabletop spotlight. There are lots of standard-voltage designs available. However, they do get extremely hot, so it is worth investing in a low-voltage version to provide a better, slightly cooler—and therefore safer—light source. Many designs allow you to add lenses and louvers to the bulb to soften the light. It is also worth experimenting to find the best position for the light. This can sometimes be in front, to the side or behind the object.

▼ **Something fishy**
An uplit fireplace balances the light used to highlight an unusual display of fish. The bulb in the overhead light source has a wide beam, creating a wash of light onto the front of these three-dimensional objects. The resulting shadows create a highly original focal point.

▲ **Textural impact**
The simplest lighting often has the most impact. This fossil is lit from overhead using a ceiling-recessed spotlight that is fitted with a narrow beam for maximum impact. The stark light enhances the texture of the fossil and its natural spiral shape.

Collections

Semi-recessed under-cabinet lights can be used to light collections of glass, china or photographs in individual niches. This is a useful device for injecting some interest into a potentially bland space. This approach works equally well in shelves used to display objects. Such lighting can act as a substitute for table or floor lamps when there is insufficient floor space. Objects placed on top of cabinets or beams and shelves can be backlit using a linear LED or a low-voltage light source.

Key tips for lighting ojects of interest

■ Experiment with a variety of positions to ensure the best result from the light source.
■ Remember that you can usually find a plug-in solution for lighting objects when built-in lighting is not an option.
■ Don't place the light source too close to the object to be lit.

▲ **Compact solution**
An alternative to lamp light in the form of under-cabinet LED light provides an attractive display for memorabilia and collectibles (top). A similar treatment (above) creates a lively focus on a half-landing.

Paintings, drawings and prints

There are several different methods you can use to light works of art hanging on your walls. Use a ceiling-recessed low-voltage adjustable spot for the best results. Low-voltage bulbs will give you the most flexibility, as you can choose from among a variety of different strengths of light and beam widths to suit your picture. Another option is a linear wall-mounted picture light (either traditional or contemporary in style). These can be fixed to the wall or to the back of a picture. If you are unsure about what style would suit the room and picture best, you can ask your electrician to install the outlet and cover it with a wall plate, to enable you to install the light fixture of your choice at a later date. Such decorative picture lights—either low voltage or standard voltage—will never light artwork as well as a ceiling-recessed picture light because they cannot produce the same amount of light. However, they can add to the atmosphere of a room.

For a really spectacular effect, use a framing projector. This low-voltage method for lighting works of art can be expensive, but it can be removed and reinstalled if you move.

Key tips for lighting pictures

Use picture lights to ensure that works of art can be viewed to their best advantage at any time of day, to create clear focal points in a room, and to provide added atmosphere and an intermediate light in room. To achieve the best effects:

■ Opt for a color-constant low-voltage bulb to render the colors of a picture accurately.
■ Fit louvers and lenses over bulbs to concentrate the light source accurately (see page 67).
■ Use the correct beam width to match the size of the picture.
■ Consider where you will position a transformer if using low-voltage picture lights. Often, an ultra-slim version can be discreetly tucked behind a picture.

▲ ▼ ▶ Art of detail
Lighting artwork is one of the easiest ways to introduce focal points in a room. In the examples above and right, purpose-designed picture lights are used. Ceiling-recessed low-voltage spotlights (below), however, often create the most effective lighting.

Glossary

Ceiling-recessed fixture Any light fixture that is recessed into a ceiling. Also called pot lights.

Color temperature A characteristic of visible light. Although most bulbs emit "white" light, this can vary from a cozy "warm" white to a "cold" white, according to the color temperature of the bulb. The temperature is conventionally stated in kelvins (K). Higher color temperatures (5,000 K or more) are called cool colors (bluish-white), and lower color temperatures are called warm colors (yellowish-white through to red).

Compact fluorescent bulb A gas-filled bulb that uses electricity to excite mercury vapor. Excited mercury atoms produce shortwave ultraviolet light that causes a phosphor coating on the inside of the bulb to produce a visible light. This type of bulb converts electrical power into useful light more efficiently than an incandescent bulb.

Dimmer A mechanism that can vary the current through an electric light in order to control the level of illumination.

Downlight A ceiling-recessed fixture, or a light fixture mounted on a ceiling, that casts light in a downward direction.

Driver A device that provides a constant current or constant voltage to an LED in order to maintain a constant light output.

Floor-recessed uplight A light fixture recessed into the floor that concentrates light in an upward direction. Generally used to create strongly defined accent light. (See also wall-mounted uplight.)

Floor washer A light fixture that is set at a low level in a wall or stair to provide a gentle wash of light to the floor or to skim light across a stair tread.

Incandescent bulb A source of electric light that works by incandescence (a general term for heat-driven light emissions). An electric current passes through a thin filament, heating it to a temperature that produces light. Also called tungsten bulb.

LED (light-emitting diode) When electricity is passed through an LED, energy is released in the form of photons. They are usually tiny (less than a thousandth of a square inch/1 mm²), and their radiation and reflection are shaped by integrated optical components. LEDs are characterized by low energy consumption, long life and fast switching. An LED is often referred to as a light "engine."

Low-voltage lighting A lighting system or product that uses a transformer to reduce the standard-voltage supply (usually 120 volts) to 12 volts.

Spotlight An adjustable (directional) light fixture, recessed into a ceiling or surface mounted, that casts light at a specific angle.

Standard-voltage supply The general alternating current (AC) electrical power supply. In the U.S., electric power is referred to by several names, including household power, household electricity, domestic power, wall power and live power. In Canada, it is often called "hydro," as much of Canada's electricity is generated by hydropower. In North America the standard voltage is 120 volts.

Switch The "on/off" control that provides power to light fixtures.

Wall-mounted uplight A light fixture on a wall that concentrates light in an upward direction. Used to provide a soft, indirect illumination to a space. (See also floor-recessed uplight.)

Resources

International Association of Lighting Designers (IALD)
(www.iald.org)
An international federation of professional lighting designers
and professional lighting consultants. Provides contact details
of members.

Professional Lighting Designers' Association
(www.pld-a.org)
An international organization, based in the U.S., of professional
lighting designers who are primarily involved in architectural lighting
design. Its aim is to promote an appreciation of the importance of
good lighting design and to uphold professional standards. It awards
prizes annually for excellence in lighting design.

Suppliers

Album srl
T: +39 (03) 9963 5452
F: +39 (03) 9596 3776
www.album.it

Anglepoise Ltd
T: +44 (0)2392 224 450
F: +44 (0)2392 385445
www.anglepoise.com

Artemide
T: +39 (02) 93518.1 – 93526.1
F: +39 (02) 93590254 – 93590496
www.artemide.com

Artemis Design Ltd
T: (312) 421 8535
F: (312) 988 7090
www.artemisdesign.net

Arturo Alvarez
T: +1 (732) 271 0700
F: +1 (732) 271 0702
www.arturo-alvarez.com

Astro Lighting
T: +44 (0)1279 427001
F: +44 (0)1279 427002
www.astrolighting.co.uk

AXO Light USA, Inc.
T: (203) 730 0452
F: (203) 730 0460
www.axolight.it

B Lux
T: +34 902 10 77 35
F: +34 902 10 77 96
www.grupoblux.com

Barovier & Toso
T: +39 (02) 7600 0906
F: +39 (02) 7640 8729
www.barovier.com

Bella Figura
T: US: (800) 453 3563
Canada: (800) 535 3258
www.bella-figura-us.com

Besselink & Jones
T: +44 (0)20 8689 9405
F: +44 (0)20 8665 0228
www.besselink.com

Best and Lloyd
T: +44 (0)20 7610 9191
F: +44 (0)20 7610 9193
www.bestandlloyd.com

Bloom Bloempot
T: +31 (0)2355 12852
F: +31 (0)2355 12853
www.bloomholland.nl

Boyd Lighting
T: +1 (415) 778 4300
F: +1 (415) 778 4319
www.boydlighting.com

Cameron Peters Fine Lighting Ltd
T: +44 (0)1235 835 000
F: +44 (0)1235 835 005
www.cameronpeters.co.uk

Christopher Wray
T: +44 (0)20 7751 8701
F: +44 (0)20 7731 3507
www.christopherwray.co.uk

CTO Lighting
T: +1 (215) 496 0440
F: +1 (215) 496 0441
www.ctolighting.co.uk

Davey Lighting Ltd
T: +44 (0)1394 386768
F: +44 (0)1394 387228
www.davey-lighting.co.uk

David Wilkinson
T: +44 (0)20 8314 1080
F: +44 (0)20 8690 1524
www.wilkinson-plc.com

Decodame
www.decodame.com

Delta Light USA
T: +1 (954) 677 9800
F: +1 (954) 677 1007
www.deltalight.com

Diffuse Limited
T: +44 (0)1462 638 331
F: +44 (0)1462 638 332
www.diffuse.co.uk

Eglo Leuchten GmbH
T: +43 5242 6996 0
F: +43 5242 6996 938
www.eglo.com

Flos
www.flos.it

Foscarini
T: +39 (04) 1595 3811
F: +39 (04) 1595 3820
www.foscarini.com

Heathfield & Co
T: +44 (0)1732 350450
www.heathfield.co.uk

Hector Finch
T: +1 (212) 935 6376
www.hectorfinch.com

Inspired by Design
T: +44 (0)161 278 2094
F: +44 (0)871 288 2843
www.inspired-by-design.co.uk

Jim Lawrence Traditional Ironwork
T: +44 (0)1473 826 685
F: +44 (0)1473 824 074
www.jim-lawrence.co.uk

John Cullen Lighting
T: +44 (0)20 7371 5400
F: +44 (0)20 7371 7799
www.johncullenlighting.co.uk

Kevin Reilly
T: +1 (773) 235 8909
www.kevinreillylighting.com

La-Lou Ltd
T: +44 (0)20 7736 0030
F: +44 (0)20 7736 8630
www.la-lou.com

Light Projects Ltd
T: +44 (0)20 7231 8282
F: +44 (0)20 7273 4342
www.lightprojects.co.uk

Louis Poulsen
T: +1 (954) 349 2525
www.louispoulsen.com

Louise Bradley
T: +44 (0)20 7589 1442
F: +44 (0)20 7751 0882
www.louisebradley.co.uk

Mathmos Ltd
T: +44 (0)20 7549 2700
F: +44 (0)20 7739 4064
www.mathmos.com

Mr. Light
T: +44 (0)20 7352 8398
F: +44 (0)20 7351 3484
www.mrlight.co.uk

Ochre
T: +1 (212) 414 4332
F: +1 (212) 219 1161
www.ochre.net

Oluce
T: +39 (02) 9849 1435
F: +39 (02) 9849 0779
www.oluce.com

Orchid
T: +44 (0)20 7384 2443
F: +44 (0)20 7013 0701
www.orchidfurniture.co.uk

Original BTC
T: +44 (0)1993 882 251
F: +44 (0)1993 882 424

Period Style Lighting
T: +44 (0)1992 554 943
www.periodstylelighting.co.uk

Porta Romana
T: +1 (305) 672 9958
F: +1 (646) 964 6669
www.portaromana.co.uk

Precision Lighting Ltd
T: +44 (0)20 8947 6616
F: +44 (0)20 8286 6626
www.precisionlighting.co.uk

Quasar Holland B.V
T: +31 183 447887
F: +31 183 448337
www.quasar.nl

Quoizel
T: +1 (631) 273 2700
F: +1 (631) 231 7102
www.quoizel.com

Rejuvenation
T: +1 (888) 401 1900
F: +1 (800) 526 7329
www.rejuvenation.com

Robert Abbey Inc
T: +1 (866) 203 5392
F: +1 (815) 366 0385
www.robertabbey.com

Sander Mulder
T: +31 (0)40 21 22 900
F: +31 (0)40 21 29 902
www.sandermulder.com

Secto Design
T: +35 8 9 505 0598
F: +35 8 9 547 52535
www.sectodesign.fi

Studio Italia Design
T: +1 (305) 621 9602
F: +1 (786) 513 3721
www.sid-usa.com

Studio/Louise Campbell
T: +45 33 11 80 06
www. louisecampbell.com

Tecnolumen
T: +49 (0) 421 430 417 – 0
F: +49 (0) 421 4986 685
www.tecnolumen.de

Terzani USA, Inc
T: +1 (954) 438 7779
F: +1 (954) 438 7566
www.terzani.com

The Conran Shop
T: +1 (866) 755 9079
F: +1 (212) 780 0060
www.conranusa.com

The English Lamp Company
T: +44 (0)1328 878 586
www.englishlampcompany.com

The Oil Lamp Store
www.theoillampstore.com

Tindle Lighting
T: +44 (0)20 7384 1485
F: +44 (0)20 7736 5630
www.tindle-lighting.co.uk

Tobias Grau
T: +49 (0)40 3003 5831
F: +49 (0)40 3003 5782
www.tobias-grau.com

Valerie Wade
T: +44 (0)20 7225 1414
www.valeriewade.com

Vaughan
T: +1 (212) 319 7070
F: +1 (212) 319 7766
www.vaughandesigns.com

Wever & Ducre
T: +32 5123 2440
F: +32 5122 9703
www.wever-ducre.com

William Yeoward
T: +44 (0)20 7349 7828
www.williamyeoward.com

Yamagiwa Usa Corporation
T: +1 (818) 879 8611
F: +1 (818) 879 8640
www.yamagiwausa.com

Zero
T: +46 (0)481 800 00
F: +46 (0)481 140 00
www.zero.se

Index

Page number in *italic* refer to illustrations

A
architectural features: highlighting 39, 232
artwork:
lighting 73–74, 84, 88, *186*, 193, *193*, 245, *245*
from ceiling spots *71*
with spots *29*, *84*, *95*, *98*
automated controls 45

B
barn conversions 80
bathrooms 20, *21*, 218–223, *218–223*
concealed lighting *112*
electrical safety 222
half baths 212–213, *212–213*
layered lighting 30, *222–223*
mirrors *118*, *119*, *219*
slots and niches *114*, 115, *115*
task lighting 125–126, *125*
up/down lights *91*
uplights in bath surround 220
beam widths *34*
bedrooms 18–20, *20*, 214–217, *214–217*
child's *200*
layering light 30
closets: lighting *71*
concealed lighting for *102*, *104*, *113*
downlighting headboard 69
niche lighting *116*, 117
reading lights 125–126,

126, 214–216, *214*
slot and niche lighting *116*, 117
task lighting 125–126, *126*
use of dimmers *217*
bedside lamps 125–126, *126*, 214–216, *214*
bulbs:
banned 22
changing 52, *53*
for spotlights 71–72
types 22–24, *22–24*, 26–27, *26–27*

C
cable systems 86–88, *86–89*
dos and don'ts 88
fixtures *86–87*
ceiling-mounted fixtures 144, *144–145*
ceilings:
dropped *108*, 111
dos and don'ts 111
lighting 109–110
CF (compact fluorescent) bulbs 26, *26*
chandelier: cross-lighting 18
children's rooms 200–201, *200–201*
fun lighting for 164, *164–165*
layering light 30
task lighting 200–201
closets: directional spots on *71*
coffer lighting *104*, 108–112, *108–113*
dos and don'ts 111
light sources 110–112
positioning 108–109
cold cathode 111
collections: lighting 244, *244*

color 23, 37
in bathrooms 220–222
in home gym 224, *225*
introducing 60–61, *60–61*
outdoors 236, 239
special effects 128–130, *128*, *129*
temperature 22, *23*
of tiles 226
concealed lighting 102–106, *102–107*
dos and don'ts 105
fixtures for *102–103*
for mirrors *120*
control systems 42–45, *45*
complete home automation 45
dimming 42–43
energy-saving 45
one-room 44
whole-house 44
wireless 44
corners: lighting 58
cove lighting 108–112, *108–113*
dos and don'ts 111
light sources 110–112
positioning 108–109
curtains *see* drapes

D
dead space: avoiding 240–242
decks *234*
desk lamps 162, *162–163*
diffused light 14
dimmers 20, 30, 61
manual 42
push-button 42–43
for staircases 182
dining rooms 18, *19*, 192–194, *192–195*

layered lighting 30, *194*
  peripheral light 193–194
dining table: lighting
  192–193, *193*
display units: lighting 72,
  85, *191*
double-height spaces 40–41,
  80, 81, 88, 89
up-down lights 95
downlights:
  beam widths *64*, 66,
    66–67
  ceiling-recesssed *14*
  dos and don'ts 68
  effects achieved with 64
  hardware *64*
  miniature *15*
  planning 66
  recessed: fixed 64–68,
    64–69
  wall-mounted *29*, 90–95
drapes: lighting *74*, 194,
  214, 240
dressing rooms 216, *216*
dressing table: lighting 217
drinks' cabinet: spotlighting
  79

E
edges: softening 104–106
energy-efficient lighting
  26–27
energy-saving bulbs 27
energy-saving controls 45
entrances 174–177, *174*

F
features: emphasizing 39
fiber-optic system 25, *25*
firehood *64*
fireplace: as focal point *98*,
  241
floor lamps 20
floor washers *29*, 40
  dos and don'ts 99
  wall-recessed 96–100,
    96–101

fixtures *96–97*
floor-recessed uplights
  96–100, *96–101*
  dos and don'ts 99
  fixtures *96–97*
floor-standing lamps:
  classic and traditional
    150, *150–151*
  contemporary 152,
    152–153
fluorescent bulbs 22, 23, *23*
  colored 23
fluorescent lights 20
  linear *38*
focal points:
  in living rooms 185–186
  in open-plan living
    197–198
  outdoors 234, *235, 239*
  picking out 175–176
framing projector: using 74
front doors: lighting
  172–173, *172–173*
fun lighting 164, *164–165*
furniture:
  adding light to 38–39
  lighting under *31, 50*, 106,
    106, 107

G
glass: lighting through 103

H
half baths 212–213,
  212–213
hallways 16, *16, 29*, 51,
  174–177, *175–177*
  dropped ceiling in *111*
  layered lighting *40*, 174,
    175
  spotlights in *77*
halogen bulbs 24, *24*
home gyms 224–225,
  224–225
home offices 20, 202–204,
  202–205

  in dual-use room 204, *204*
house facade: uplighting *172*

I
incandescent bulbs 22, *22*
  for uplights 79
IRC bulbs 26, 79

K
kick plate: lights in *99, 191*
kids' lighting 164, *164–165*
kitchens 16–18, *18, 85*,
  188–191, *188–191*
  adapting existing scheme
    38–39, *38*
  cable spotlights in 86, *87*
  floor-washers 99, 191
  layering light sources
    33–37, 41
  plans *32*
  task lighting *125*, 188,
    189–190, *189*

L
landings 178, *179, 180*,
  181–182
  positioning controls
    181–182
laundry rooms 207
layered lighting 16, 17, *28*,
  30, *30–37*
  adapting existing scheme
    38–39
  plans *32*
  separating layers 40–41
LEDs 25, *25*, 27
  colored 112
  flexible 20
  for floor lighting 100
  for spots 75
  for stairwell *183*
  strip *21*
  in track lighting 84
lenses 67 light:
  magic of 8
  understanding 14–15

light sources:
  choosing 22–25
  controlling 42–45
  layering 30, *30–37*
  plug-in 58–59
  positioning 28–29
lighting:
  energy-efficient 26–27
  ≠of future 8–9
  good: fundamentals 9
  improving existing system
  46–61
  to suit rooms 16–21
  surface-mounted 76–81
linear lighting: concealed 31,
36, 37
living rooms 16, *17,* 184–187
layered lighting *28,* 187
  mirrors in *122, 123*
loft conversions 80
lofts 41 louvers 67
lumens 23

M
media rooms 208–211,
208–211
control system 210–211
double use 210, *210*
mirror lighting 14, 74–75,
118–122, *118–123*
  backlighting 220
  concealed *120*
  dos and don'ts 122
  in dressing rooms 216
  fixtures 118–119
  in half baths 212, *212*
mood: light and 10, 15

N
narrow spaces 84–85
natural light 48–51
niche lighting 20, *21,*
114–117, *114–116*
  dos and don'ts 117
  downlights *65,* 68
night-lights *97,* 100, *101*

O
objects:
  cross-lighting *114*
  downlights on 65
  lighting 58, 243, *243*
  open-plan living spaces 40,
  196–198, *196–199*
    layered lighting 197,
    198–199
    lighting circuits 196–197
    positioning controls 198
    visual dividers 197
outdoors 234–239, *234–239*
  colored effects *133*
  electrical safety 239
  fixtures for 234–236
  layered lighting *235,* 237
  slot lighting 117, *117*
  swimming pools 228, *229*
  weatherproof fixtures 168,
  168–169

P
patio garden *29*
pendants:
  classic 136, *136–137*
  contemporary 138,
  138–141
  traditional 142, *142–143*
picture lights 166, *166–167*
pitched roof 40, *89*
planning: for future changes
240
plants: lighting *237, 238, 239*
playroom 20
  doubling as media room
  210
  lighting 200, *201*
  plug-in lights 58–59
  LED uplights *100*
porch lighting 232
porches: lighting 172–173,
172–173

R
reading lights 18–20,
125–126, *126, 127*
  around sofa 184, *184*
reflection: using 9, 14
restricted space: lighting
179–180
roof light *49*
rooms: lighting to suit 16–21

S
safety tips 61
sculpture: lighting *78, 94*
shades:
  changing 54–57
  choosing 55
  color 27
  shape and size 56, *57*
shadow:
  avoiding: on mirrors 120
  importance of 10, 14–15
shelving: concealed lighting
103–104, *103, 104, 105*
showers:
  concealed lighting 102
  downlighting *77,* 218–220
  niches in *220*
  obscuring *221*
sketches *30*
sky effects *130, 131,*
132–133, 208–209
skylights 50, *86*
slot lighting 114–117,
114–117
  dos and don'ts 117
sofa: lighting 184–185
special-effects lighting
128–133, *128–133*
  dos and don'ts 133
split-level apartments 41
spotlights *17*
  beam widths *70*
  bulbs for 71–72
  ceiling-recessed 18, *18*
  choosing fixtures 70–71
  directional 14, *15,* 18
  dos and don'ts 72

fixtures *70–71*
  positioning 72
  recessed 70–75, *70–75*
  using lenses 73
finishes 65
LEDs for *75*
low-voltage *79*
  transformer for 79
on pictures *29, 84, 95, 98*
on roof beams 40
surface-mounted 76–79, *77*
stair wells 181–182
staircases *40*, 41, 178–183
  dimmers 182
  lighting handrail 179, *179*
  lighting tight turns 85
  positioning controls
  181–182
slot lighting 115–117
step washers 96, *96, 100,*
174, 180, 181
  to wine cellar 206
standard lamps 16
starlight effects 230
steps: lighting 209–210
stove hood *190*
study 20
sunrooms 230–233,
230–233
  linking with outdoors *231,*
232, 233
surface-mounted lighting
76–80, *76–81*
  dos and don'ts 80
  fixtures *76–77*
  tips 80
swimming pools 226–228,
226–229
switches 42–43, *42–43*

T
table lamps 16, *16*, 20
  classic 154, *154–155*
  contemporary 156,
156–159
  traditional 160, *160–161*
task lighting 20, 35,

124–127, *124–127*
  for children 200–201
  dos and don'ts 126
  fixtures *124–125*
  for home office 202–204,
202–204
  in kitchen 125, 188, *188,*
189–190
texture: highlighting *29, 75,*
243
tiles:
  downlighting 65
  reflecting light off *101*
toe kick *see* kick plate
track lighting 82–85, *82–85*
  choosing 82–84
  fixtures *82–83*
  low-voltage 82–83
  transformer: positioning
  79, 82–83
trees: lighting 236

U
up/down lights 90–95,
90–95
  dos and don'ts 92
uplights:
  on beams 40, *78*, 79
  behind object *15*
  floor-recessed *21*, 96–100,
96–101
  fixtures *96–97*
  in ground *29*
  LED *100*
  low-voltage 39
  surface-mounted *78,*
79–80
  wall-mounted 14, 90–95
utility room 20

V
vanity:
  light under *218*
  lighting 212, *213*

W
wall lights *17*, 18, 18
  classic/traditional 148,
148–149
  contemporary 146,
146–147
  downlights 90–95, *90–95*
  swing-arm 185
  uplights 90–95, *90–95*
water feature: highlighting
237
waterfall control *44*
watts 23
windows *48*
  at night 50, *50*
  spotlighting *74*, 75
  on staircases 180
  uplighting *97*, 194
wine cellars 206–207,
206–207
working space: lighting
124–125, *124*

Y
yards 234–239, *234, 238,*
239
  fixtures for 234–236

Credits

Quarto would like to thank the following for kindly supplying images for inclusion in this book:

a = above; b = bottom; c = center; l = left; r = right; t = top.

p.11, 59t, 72, 73, 93, 127, 184, 189 **Louise Bradley Interiors**

p.16, 44, 67, 107t, 112, 132, 185, 203 **AJB Interiors**

p.16, 44, 61, 67, 87, 107t, 112, 132, 185, 203, 208, 221, 236 **Luke White Photography**

p.17 **Carnegie Club/Victoria Fairfax Interiors**

p.19, 68, 115, 116t, 119, 199, 243, 244t **Claire Williams Interiors**

p.19, 40, 68, 115, 116t, 119, 179r, 182, 191, 199, 202, 218, 219b, 228, 243, 244 **Andrew Beasley Photography**

p.21t, 71, 178, 186, 187, 195, 200, 201, 210, 211, 217, 220b, 224/244b **LBR Interiors**

p.25 **Roblon**

p.29b, 42, 43 49t, 51, 86, 91t, 92b, 107b, 109, 117, 125, 173, 180r, 181, 183l, 197, 213t, 219t, 235, 237, 238, 239 **James Cameron Photography**

p.29t, 237 **Charlotte Rowe Garden Design**

p.21b **Vivien Lawrence Design**

p.29b, 175 **Sarah King Designs**

p.31, 50, 54b, 105l, 213b **Taylor Howes Designs**

p.42–43b **Forbes & Lomax www.forbesandlomax.com**

p.45cm, 45bc **Crestron**

p.45bl **Rako Controls**

p.45ar, 61 **Lutron**

p.45al/br **iLight**

p.53 all lamps from **Christopher Wray**

p.55t **Louis Poulsen**

p.55br **Heathfield**

p.58 **FLOS**

p.60 **www.encapsulite.com**

p.67, 82–83, 84–85 **Precision Lighting**

p.69, 92t, 220 **Stephen Fletcher Architects**

p.78, 207 **Alison Henry Design**

p.87l **Ingo Maurer**

p.87tr, 208, 216, 221 **Todhunter Earle**

p.227 **The Interior Company**

p.95 **Studio Azzuro**

p.111 **Sylvia Lawson Johnson**

p.172 **Tim Street Porter**

p.174 **Arcaid**

p.229t **Corbis**

p.231t **Red Cover**

p.232b **Alamy**

Quarto would also like to thank the manufacturers and designers, credited in the captions, who supplied photographs of the light fixtures featured in Part 4. Contact details are listed under Suppliers. Special thanks are due to Cameron Peters for the supply of images.

All other images are the copyright of Quarto Publishing plc. While every effort has been made to credit contributors, Quarto would like to apologize should there have been any omissions or errors, and would be pleased to make the appropriate correction for future editions of the book.

Project Editor: Cathy Meeus
Art Editor: Moira Clinch
Designer: Karin Skånberg

Picture researchers: Sarah Bell and Sarah Rober
Photographer: Phil Wilkins
Illustrator: John Woodcock
Art Director: Caroline Guest
Proofreader: Claire Waite Brown
Indexer: Dorothy Frame

Invaluable assistance from Corinne Masciocchi,
Sally Bond and Susi Martin

Creative Director: Moira Clinch
Publisher: Paul Carslake